DEFENDING YOUR TESTIMONY IN THE LATTER DAYS

BE YE WISE AS SERPENTS

DEFENDING YOUR TESTIMONY IN THE LATTER DAYS

BE YE WISE AS SERPENTS

SCOTT R. FRAZER

CFI
An imprint of Cedar Fort, Inc.
Springville, Utah

Paperback ISBN 13: 978-1-4621-4571-3
Ebook ISBN 13: 978-1-4621-3127-3

Published by CFI, an imprint of Cedar Fort, Inc.
2373 W. 700 S., Suite 100 Springville, UT 84663
Distributed by Cedar Fort, Inc., www.cedarfort.com

Library of Congress Registration Number: 2023941145

Cover design by Shawnda Craig
Cover design © 2023 Cedar Fort, Inc.
Edited and typeset by Valene Wood

Printed in the United States of America

10 9 8 7 6 5 4 3 2 1

Printed on acid-free paper

I would like to dedicate this book to my grandchildren. More than any other living generation, theirs will need the wisdom of the serpent and the spirituality of the dove to meet the challenges of Earth life.

Enoch, Tyson, & Eden Frazer, Owen, Everly, Archer, & Olive Clune, Claire, Eleanor, & Audrey Frazer and any grandchildren yet unborn, I hope you will read this book and have awesome lives.
May God bless you.

Other books by Scott R. Frazer:

Where Science Meets God: 12 Ways Science Reinforces LDS Doctrine

Angry with God: Understanding the Rules of Earth Life

Mentally Calm, Spiritually Connected: The Interdependence of Mind and Spirit

Contents

Introduction

In general, members of The Church of Jesus Christ of Latter-day Saints are very nice and trusting people. This is a good thing . . . usually. However, as He sent out His apostles to be missionaries, the Savior warned them to *not* be naïve nor blind to the deceptions of men. The title of this book is taken from that verse, found in Matthew 10:16.

> Behold, I send you forth as sheep in the midst of wolves: be ye therefore wise as serpents, and harmless as doves.

This is excellent advice, not only for a team of apostles heading out on their missions, but for Christians worldwide. In fact, these might have been the exact instructions we were given as we left the premortal existence and came to Earth. By choosing these two extreme similes, the Savior summarizes how His followers must deal with the outside world. First, consider the dove—harmless, innocent, and gentle. The dove is a symbol of peace and love. A dove's coo is calming; mothers are said to coo their babies to sleep. Church members are taught to attain such caring, empathetic attitudes, and there are many dovelike members in The Church of Jesus Christ of Latter-day Saints. A dove is always caring, optimistic, and even spiritual—attitudes that are often difficult to maintain in an increasingly selfish world. This approach to others seems to be at the core of Church teachings.

So, why did the Savior command us to be wise as serpents as well? Because, as He states, He knew His apostles (and other faithful followers) were going out into the world like sheep into the midst of wolves. To get the correct image in your head, a sheep in the midst of wolves doesn't last long. It's ripped to shreds and devoured. The Savior knew that the members of His church couldn't be doves all the time—or they would suffer similar fates.

Let's consider the serpent. Normally, serpents are thought to be evil and calculating, such as the serpent we find in the Garden of Eden. However, Jesus Christ also uses the serpent as a simile of how the apostles needed to be. The serpent is wise in the ways of the world, careful, untrusting, and suspicious. The serpent is a symbol of being "street smart" and being nobody's fool. While it is easy to scam a dove, you can't scam a serpent. The Savior could have used a simile other than a serpent to illustrate how we should be wise. He could have used an owl, a fox, or even a wise man. Instead, he encouraged us to have the wisdom of the serpent, which is shrewd, cautious, and unwilling to mince words. The serpent is suspicious because, in general, snakes are hated by men. Most of us have an inexplicable, deep-seated fear of snakes. Men will often kill a snake when they come upon it—even if it is non-poisonous and harmless. Serpents must be untrusting of men, because if they aren't, they die.

The serpent's approach to life and worship is practical, more academic, and less soft-hearted. The Savior purposefully chose two symbols that are extremes, yet He wants you to be a mixture of both. The Church needs members to protect it from the evils of the world. Doves can be naïve, and the days are past when Latter-day Saints can be naïve in the ways of the world. Years ago, in my student ward at the University of Arizona, a newly arrived young man named Jonathan decided to be baptized into the Church. Of course, everyone in the ward was thrilled and wanted to help Jonathan out. One ward member loaned him a car. Others loaned him cash. Yet another loaned him an expensive camera. Less than two weeks later, Jonathan disappeared with everything. This was a harsh lesson for those who had trusted this young man. They had tried to do good but were robbed in their efforts. Loaning your car to a veritable stranger is kind, but dangerous.

There are plenty of sayings to reflect this dichotomy of being faithful yet practical. One attributed to Saint Augustine is, "Pray as though everything depended on God. Work as though everything depended on you." A newer adage might be, "Have faith that God will spare your life, but still buy life insurance." The Savior even had one of His own. "Which of you shall have an ass or an ox fallen into a pit, and will not straightway pull him out on the sabbath day?" (Luke 14:5). In other words, faith alone will not get your ox out of a pit on the Sabbath. In early Church history, missionaries could go out "without purse or script." Today, our missionaries don't do that. The Church needed to adopt a more practical approach to missionary work in a new world.

In my discussion about doves and serpents, my purpose will not be to hold one above the other. Christians need to be both. Yet it appears that many members in The Church of Jesus Christ of Latter-day Saints have forgotten all about the need to be serpents. It is a bad time to make such a choice. The world is becoming a dangerous place indeed. The Church is under attack by those who deceive in order to convince our young adult members to leave the

Church. They seek to demoralize our young men and women from preparing for their missions. We cannot deal with these threats as doves, because doves are simply not tough enough to handle the challenge.

Perhaps a couple of examples are in order, starting with church welfare. The duty to oversee church welfare is one of the most difficult responsibilities of Church leadership. The needy family expects their ward leaders to be dovelike, as they are in church meetings. However, Church leaders understand that, if church welfare was provided to every member who desired it, our religion would soon go bankrupt. Thus, local authorities must follow very serpentlike guidelines as to how much welfare they can distribute.

Equating dovelike personalities as being tenderhearted and serpentlike qualities as being tough-minded, Dr. Martin Luther King gave a speech entitled "A Tough Mind and a Tender Heart." Drawing his sermon from this book's signature verse, "Be ye therefore wise as serpents, and harmless as doves" (Matthew 10:16), Dr. King warned us against being either soft-minded or hard-hearted.

> Rarely do we find men who willingly engage in hard, solid thinking. There is an almost universal quest for easy answers and half-baked solutions. Nothing pains some people more than having to think. . . .
>
> . . . Our minds are constantly being invaded by legions of half-truths, prejudices, and false facts. One of the great needs of mankind is to be lifted above the morass of false propaganda. . . . But we must not stop with the cultivation of a tough mind. The gospel also demands a tender heart. . . . The hardhearted individual lacks the capacity for genuine compassion. . . .
>
> Jesus reminds us that the good life combines the toughness of the serpent and the tenderness of the dove. To have serpentlike qualities devoid of dovelike qualities is to be passionless, mean, and selfish. To have dovelike without serpentlike qualities is to be sentimental, anemic, and aimless.[1]

The Reason for this Book

You may be wondering what has changed in the world such that faithful Church members need to be more serpentlike. These changes were illustrated to me in what started out as a normal stake meeting.

A few months ago, I attended a Saturday evening session of our stake conference. Our area representative, mission president, and temple president were all in attendance. The area rep led a discussion about "How to

Make our Homes into Missionary Training Centers" to prepare our young men and women for missions. Soon we had a couple dozen answers on the white board—play Church music in the home, have family prayer, read the scriptures together, and discuss the workings of the Spirit. All very good—and very dovelike—answers. Then the mission president raised his hand. His comment went something like this,

> The top things I have to worry about with new missionaries is their anxiety, their depression, masturbation, and viewing pornography. I think parents need to have more serious and difficult conversations with their sons before their missions. Don't be afraid to check the viewing history on their phones—because we will do so when they are in the mission field.

There was a shocked silence in the chapel for several seconds. Were parents worried about playing Church music in their homes and not about their son's mental health and possible pornography addiction? We had just been exposed to a very disturbing and serpentlike reality. Most of us had no idea that things had gotten this bad.

The area authority then changed the discussion topic to "Preparing our Youth for the Temple." Again, the white board was soon filled with many of the same suggestions as before—make your home like the temple, play Tabernacle Choir music, discuss the meaning of covenants, etc. Then the temple president interjected something like the following.

> Parents, you need to tell your sons and daughters exactly what to expect in their first temple visit. Explain the initiatory washing, anointing, and clothing ordinances and the meaning of each item of the temple clothing. Review the endowment. We have far too many people coming out of their first temple visit visibly shaken and disturbed.

In support of this statement, the area authority then read a quote by Elder David Bednar that gave the very *short* list of what aspects of the temple should *not* be discussed outside of the temple.[2] For the second time that evening the congregation was momentarily silenced by a serpentlike truth. Temple ordinances are challenging to understand. Our youth have been told by social media that Church members make strange, cult-like promises there. One's first temple visit can be so strange that young adults may come to believe what they have read on the internet. Parents should no longer assume that their children "will be just fine" in their first temple experience.

Our young people need to be taught step-by-step what will happen in the temple and what each step symbolizes before they enter it.

In conclusion, the dovelike attitude that our sons and daughters are prepared for their missions and temple ordinances *without needing to have difficult discussions with their parents* is not true today. The world has changed. There is so much misinformation being distributed by so many outlets, that parents must bolster their communication and oversight. Past generations were able to enjoy the luxury of being doves most of the time. In those simpler times, our society still supported a belief in God and weekly church attendance. Today, such beliefs are the exception, not the rule. As Church members, we need to apply our serpent sides to facing our problems—directly, unflinchingly, and with brutal honesty. There are very good reasons why the Savior told us to be wise as serpents, and even better reasons why we must heed that advice today.

Do Not Fear—We Knew This Was Coming

Throughout the scriptures the Lord warns us of the latter days. A good example of such a verse is found in the first section of the Doctrine and Covenants (D&C). Section 1 "constitutes the Lord's preface to the doctrines, covenants, and commandments given in this dispensation." It's rather like a summary of the rest of the scripture. Speaking of those who will not hear the voice of the Lord, we read,

> For they have strayed from mine ordinances, and have broken mine everlasting covenant;
>
> They seek not the Lord to establish his righteousness, but every man walketh in his own way, and after the image of his own god, whose image is in the likeness of the world . . . (D&C 1:15–16)

Yet, we also find messages of hope and promises throughout the scriptures. One of my favorites is also found in Doctrine and Covenants, section 18.

> Wherefore, if you shall build up my church, upon the foundation of my gospel and my rock, the gates of hell shall not prevail against you. (D&C 18:5)

This book is meant to warn and prepare us for the present-day fulfillment of dire predictions we find in the scriptures. Yet, this discussion is not meant to depress. Just like the verses quoted above, scriptural warnings are almost always followed by promises of wisdom and power. This is not accidental placement by the Lord or His prophets. God wants His children to be hopeful and faithful. But to do that—to not fear the present or future—we must be prepared. In our present day, we need to know the answers to the attacks and criticisms of the Church, so we can defend not only our own testimonies, but those of whom we love.

PART 1

Wisdom of the Serpent

Chapter 1

The Need to Be Serpents

THROUGHOUT THEIR HISTORY, CHRISTIAN CHURCHES HAVE OFTEN *NOT* followed the Savior's edict to be wise as serpents. In its earliest days of Christianity, followers did not try to maintain a low profile. Instead, missionaries preached that the Roman people should not worship the Roman gods. Consequently, Christians were branded as insurgents, which led to their imprisonment and, reportedly, being fed to lions in the Roman Coliseum. A more serpentlike and subtle approach to missionary work had to be implemented for the church to survive.

Centuries later, the Catholic Church built isolated monasteries in northern England. Monasteries were purposefully built away from cities, partly to allow monks to focus on their worship.

However, being built away from populated areas also meant these monasteries were unprotected. In AD 793, the monastery on the remote island of Lindisfarne off the coast of Northumbria was the first to be sacked and plundered by the Vikings. Such raids continued as isolated monasteries were easy pickings for raiders from the Northland. The monks who were killed in these raids almost certainly expected to be protected by God. Had they been wise as serpents, they would have known that such expectations are naïve. That is not how earth life works and there are plenty of examples to prove it.

Persecutions of Christians are found throughout all of history and across the whole earth. Millions of Christians have been killed by their governments, non-Christian religions, and even other Christian sects with slightly differing beliefs. The religious faithful undoubtedly wondered what they or their families had done to deserve being exiled, beaten, or killed. In truth, most of them had done nothing to deserve their abuse. Like the Saints who fled Nauvoo, many oppressed Christian groups have fled their homes to avoid eradication. It was a sad departure, but as the serpent would remind us, much better than the alternative.

Today, members of The Church of Jesus Christ of Latter-day Saints apparently still don't listen to their serpent side either. Utah has long been known as the fraud capital of the United States, a veritable mecca for con artists.[3] Why is this so? First, strong dovelike tendencies lead many members to trust the sincerity of strangers, making it hard to recognize when someone is lying. Secondly, Church members are well networked within their wards and stakes. When one person is told of a "fantastic investment opportunity," others soon hear about it as well. We live in a time where being naïve will not get you killed . . . but it can cause you to lose a lot of money.

Any serpent can tell you that, "If it sounds too good to be true, then it probably is." Yet many people simply don't listen their serpent side, don't check their facts, and thus choose to learn by sad experience.

Is it a Commandment to Be Wise?

The Lord's counsel to be wise as the serpent should probably be considered a commandment. The commandment to seek wisdom is mentioned so often in the scriptures that we may barely register it.

> And see that all these things are done in wisdom and order; for it is not requisite that a man should run faster than he has strength. (Mosiah 4:27)

> Seek not for riches but for wisdom, and behold, the mysteries of God shall be unfolded unto you, and then shall you be made rich. (D&C 6:7; repeated word for word in D&C 11:7)

> I tell you these things because of your prayers; wherefore, treasure up wisdom in your bosoms . . . (D&C 38:30)

> Let him that is ignorant learn wisdom by humbling himself and calling upon the Lord his God . . . (D&C 136:32)

Should we consider this counsel to be simple encouragements by the Savior to learn wisdom? Or do all these verses, taken as a whole, constitute a commandment? The Lord taught not one, but three parables about the need to be wise. Please note that one of the messages in all these parables is to not be foolish! No identifiable sins are committed in them, only foolish acts. The first, comparing the wise man who built his house on a rock with the foolish man who didn't, is found in the seventh chapter of Matthew.

> Therefore whosoever heareth these sayings of mine, and doeth them, I will liken him unto a wise man, which built his house upon a rock:
>
> And the rain descended, and the floods came, and the winds blew, and beat upon that house; and it fell not: for it was founded upon a rock.
>
> And every one that heareth these sayings of mine, and doeth them not, shall be likened unto a foolish man, which built his house upon the sand:
>
> And the rain descended, and the floods came, and the winds blew, and beat upon that house; and it fell: and great was the fall of it. (Matthew 7:24–27)

This parable equates not listening and obeying the Savior's teachings with building a house upon the sand. Fools do not recognize many of the important things of life—like following the Lord or building a house on a solid foundation. This parable tries to show us the importance of learning the Lord's teachings and using them as a foundation in our lives.

The other two parables about being wise are both found in Matthew 25. First, we read the parable of the ten virgins.

> Then shall the kingdom of heaven be likened unto ten virgins, which took their lamps, and went forth to meet the bridegroom.
>
> And five of them were wise, and five were foolish.
>
> They that were foolish took their lamps, and took no oil with them:
>
> But the wise took oil in their vessels with their lamps.
>
> While the bridegroom tarried, they all slumbered and slept.
>
> And at midnight there was a cry made, Behold, the bridegroom cometh; go ye out to meet him.
>
> Then all those virgins arose, and trimmed their lamps.
>
> And the foolish said unto the wise, Give us of your oil; for our lamps are gone out.
>
> But the wise answered, saying, Not so; lest there be not enough for us and you: but go ye rather to them that sell, and buy for yourselves.
>
> And while they went to buy, the bridegroom came; and they that were ready went in with him to the marriage: and the door was shut.
>
> Afterward came also the other virgins, saying, Lord, Lord, open to us.

> But he answered and said, Verily I say unto you, I know you not.
>
> Watch therefore, for ye know neither the day nor the hour wherein the Son of man cometh. (Matthew 25:1–13)

These five wise virgins had a very serpentlike wisdom about them. First, they were practical enough to bring extra oil in vessels with their lamps. Then, when the five foolish virgins asked for some of their oil, the five wise virgins refused them. "Not so; lest there be not enough for us!" they replied. Theirs was a very practical and wise assessment of what was necessary to be admitted into the marriage. Essentially, the wise virgins replied to the foolish virgins, "Your lack of planning is not my emergency." Once again, we have multiple meanings. Be wise, carry extra oil, and be ready for the Savior when He returns.

Immediately after the virgins' parable, we read the parable of the talents—which once again reinforces the commandment to be wise.

> For the kingdom of heaven is as a man travelling into a far country, who called his own servants, and delivered unto them his goods.
>
> And unto one he gave five talents, to another two, and to another one; to every man according to his several ability; and straightway took his journey. (Matthew 25:14–15)

The first two servants traded with their master's money and doubled his investment. But the third servant buried the one talent he was given and made nothing. To the first two servants, the lord stated, "Well done, thou good and faithful servant: thou hast been faithful over a few things, I will make thee ruler over many things: enter thou into the joy of thy lord" (Matthew 25:23). The third servant was not so congratulated.

> Then he which had received the one talent came and said, Lord, I knew thee that thou art an hard man, reaping where thou hast not sown, and gathering where thou hast not strawed:
>
> And I was afraid, and went and hid thy talent in the earth: lo, there thou hast that is thine.
>
> His lord answered and said unto him, Thou wicked and slothful servant, thou knewest that I reap where I sowed not, and gather where I have not strawed:
>
> Thou oughtest therefore to have put my money to the exchangers, and then at my coming I should have received mine own with usury. (Matthew 25:24–27)

The lord calls his unprofitable servant both *wicked* and *slothful*. Is it a sin to bury money in the ground? No, not exactly, but apparently a lack of wisdom does *not* get you into the "joy of thy Lord" either. From his own admission, the unprofitable servant knew that his lord expected a profit on the one talent he was given. He was either too foolish or lazy to figure out how to secure that profit.

The parable concludes,

> And cast ye the unprofitable servant into outer darkness: there shall be weeping and gnashing of teeth. (Matthew 25:30)

Outside of being a poor investor, the servant could have been a righteous man. But from these three parables, it seems apparent that God expects us to be wise. He is not referring only to knowledge of the gospel and scriptures. Taking these three parables in order, it seems that the Lord wants men who understand the basics of construction, women who are prepared, and servants who know something about financial investment. Admittedly, I may be taking these parables a little too literally in making my point. However, the Savior chose parables that teach us to apply wisdom in everyday matters. The Lord expects wisdom in all you do.

The Word "Christlike" Does Not Only Mean "Dovelike"

The word "Christlike" obviously means being like Christ. However, over many years, the definition of the word has drifted to mean "dovelike." Indeed, it appears that our interpretation of Christlike has drifted well beyond what the scriptures actually teach about the Savior.

For example, in the 1990s, the question, "What Would Jesus Do?", or its acronym WWJD, became very popular in religious circles. Bracelets and necklaces with WWJD embroidered or stamped on them were widespread. The assumption was that, in handling a difficult person, the Savior would always be kind, non-judgmental, and forgiving—and that we all should try to be such a person as well. This depiction defines the Savior as being a very one-dimensional being, responding to *everyone* in one predictable and lenient way. In reality, how could anyone know how Jesus would respond to a specific individual? His response would depend completely upon the person in question. The Lord may as easily condemn the person, as He did the scribes and Pharisees throughout the *entire chapter* of Matthew 23. Verses 13 and 14 are especially harsh.

> But woe unto you, scribes and Pharisees, hypocrites! for ye shut up the kingdom of heaven against men: for ye neither go in yourselves, neither suffer ye them that are entering to go in.
>
> Woe unto you, scribes and Pharisees, hypocrites! for ye devour widows' houses, and for a pretence make long prayer: therefore ye shall receive the greater damnation.

Or Jesus might both teach and call the person to repentance as He did with the Samaritan woman at Jacob's well (John 4). Or He might indeed be non-judgmental, as He was with the woman caught in adultery (John 8).

The idea that being Christlike means only being dovelike is simply not supported in the scriptures. Do you remember the account of Jesus cleansing the temple? In John 2, we read,

> And the Jews' passover was at hand, and Jesus went up to Jerusalem,
>
> And found in the temple those that sold oxen and sheep and doves, and the changers of money sitting:
>
> And when he had made a scourge of small cords, he drove them all out of the temple, and the sheep, and the oxen; and poured out the changers' money, and overthrew the tables; (John 2:13–15)

That doesn't seem very . . . dovelike. When the Savior needed to be the serpent and make His point, He did. Another good example of the Lord being very clear about a teaching is given in Matthew 18. Jesus had just invited a child to come to the center of His group of listeners. He remarked that anyone who helps one of God's children would be blessed. Then He continues with a warning to those who might do otherwise.

> But whoso shall offend one of these little ones which believe in me, it were better for him that a millstone were hanged about his neck, and that he were drowned in the depth of the sea. (Matthew 18:6)

The Lord did not sugarcoat this declaration at all. It was reputed that the Mafia used similar techniques in dealing with traitors in their organization. Yet drowning would be *better* than what would happen to you if you were to offend one of Jesus Christ's little ones. It seems the Savior is a bit protective of His children. What the Savior said here was entirely appropriate, well-spoken . . . and very serpentlike.

Repentance for Being Foolish

If it is a commandment to be wise, then shouldn't we repent when we are unwise? Such repentance doesn't seem to happen very often. The Church has produced a video called, "Where Justice, Love, and Mercy Meet"[4] that I highly recommend. It is based on a story told by Jeffrey R. Holland in the April 2015 General Conference. Elder Holland does a great job of telling this story, so I will simply quote his words.

> Without safety ropes, harnesses, or climbing gear of any kind, two brothers—Jimmy, age 14, and John, age 19 (though those aren't their real names)—attempted to scale a sheer canyon wall in Snow Canyon State Park in my native southern Utah. Near the top of their laborious climb, they discovered that a protruding ledge denied them their final few feet of ascent. They could not get over it, but neither could they now retreat from it. They were stranded. After careful maneuvering, John found enough footing to boost his younger brother to safety on top of the ledge. But there was no way to lift himself. The more he strained to find finger or foot leverage, the more his muscles began to cramp.
>
> Panic started to sweep over him, and he began to fear for his life. Unable to hold on much longer, John decided his only option was to try to jump vertically in an effort to grab the top of the overhanging ledge.
>
> Before trying this desperate maneuver, John decided to say a prayer. He begins, "Heavenly Father, I'm so sorry . . ."[5]

At this point in the video, I was moved to tears. In many Church talks, I have heard speakers relate the prayers that they offered up when they found themselves in a desperate or dangerous situation. Yet, I don't remember any of them starting out their prayer with, "Father, I'm so sorry." Yet, prayers of this nature really *should* begin with those very words.

Maybe it's because Christians think that repentance is only for apologizing for our *unrighteous* acts. Or it might be because we hate to admit when we have done something foolish. We have a host of great excuses, starting with "I didn't know!" or "It's not my fault!". But when we find ourselves in any situation for which we need to pray for help from God, we might consider beginning the prayer with something like,

> Dear Heavenly Father, I am in a desperate situation, and I need Your help. I am sorry for my part in getting myself into this predicament. I have made unwise decisions which helped create this mess. I see that now, and I ask Thy forgiveness.

Let's face it—most of our predicaments are caused, in part, by our own decisions. Throughout my career, I often found myself praying that I could find a new job. My job at the times of such prayers had not turned out as I had expected. Whose fault was that? Though I wanted to put the blame on someone else, I had accepted those jobs. The fault was mine and I had to accept that responsibility. The Lord was very patient with me during those days.

Drawing again on the above story, John and Jimmy had not actually sinned by climbing the cliff wall in Snow Canyon. But they had made a very poor decision and had put their lives in serious danger. Many other young people have died from making far less reckless decisions. The beginning of John's prayer was very appropriate. By the way, the story has a happy ending.

John made the vertical leap—and his younger brother Jimmy was there to catch him and pull him up to safety. The brothers walked away as wiser young men.

The fact that God wants you to learn wisdom should not be surprising. A big part of the reason for dividing people up into separate kingdoms at the end of mortal life is to sort out those who can be trusted with priesthood power. God doesn't want to share power with an unrighteous person, who will use it for his or her own purposes. However, God also does not want to give His power to a foolish person, who will unthinkingly misuse it. I have known kind, faithful members of the Church for whom I would throw open the gates of the celestial kingdom. But I would not wish to endow them with power, not for many years at least. Their lives on Earth were a mess due to an ongoing string of poor decisions. As Spiderman's Uncle Ben said, "With great power comes great responsibility." If someone cannot be trusted with great responsibility, he or she should not be given great power. Thus, the Lord encourages us to learn wisdom, so we are able to accept great responsibilities.

To conclude, Jesus Christ was a healthy combination of dove and serpent—and He wants us to follow His example. To follow that example, we need to be willing to be serpentlike when the situation demands it. When exactly do we have to be like serpents in our judgments? I can think of only two places—inside the home and outside it.

Chapter 2

The Wisdom of the Serpent Inside our Homes

One of the characteristics of the serpent mentioned earlier was its understanding of the ways of the world. There may be a few places on Earth today that are infallible sanctuaries from outside influences. However, such havens are extremely rare and . . . your home is probably not one of them. Parents try hard to create a bubble around their homes, as well they should. Yet, if you listen to it, the serpent part of your brain recognizes that there are many leaks in your bubble that allow temptations and evil influences into your house. Facebook, Twitter, Instagram, and other social media function as needed social outlets for your family. E-mail, texts, network television, Netflix, and other internet sites provide desired information, communication, and entertainment. Yet these sites also offer invitations to your family to stray from the covenant path. Your home has been compromised and recognizing that fact is the first step towards assessing the damage that is being incurred on your family.

Assessing your Family

Your children's Primary teachers may have assured you that your kids are a delight to teach. Your teenagers' youth leaders probably told you what great adolescents they are. The dove in you agrees wholeheartedly, thinking your children are youth of Zion with a firm grasp of the iron rod. You are certain the Spirit resides in your home. Your dove may assure you that all is well in Zion. However, that very phrase should set off alarms in your head. We read in 2 Nephi 28,

> And others will he pacify, and lull them away into carnal security, that they will say: All is well in Zion; yea, Zion prospereth, all is well—and thus the devil cheateth their souls, and leadeth them away carefully down to hell. . . .
>
> Therefore, wo be unto him that is at ease in Zion!
>
> Wo be unto him that crieth: All is well! (2 Nephi 28:21, 24–25)

Those who think that all is well in Zion are not sinning. They are simply naïve as to what is actually going on in the world. They are looking at their families through the eyes of a dove, seeing contentment, spirituality, and peace. It's what we all want to see after all. Into such a family, a parent may not see the need for having those uncomfortable, privacy-invading discussions with their teenagers. Yet Church leaders are telling parents that such discussions are needed, and woe unto those who don't follow their counsel.

The serpent within you should be very uncomfortable with your most cozy conclusions. Knowing the ways of the world, your serpent realizes that everyone is influenced by worldly temptations and that this is no time to be naïve about it. The only way to know which temptations are causing your children problems is to ask them. Your youth may deny that anything is a problem and reassure you that all is well. You might explain that you have tried to make your home a sanctuary, but in a world this chaotic, you can't be certain. Ask questions that encompass the full range of unseemly behavior for a youth of the Church. Your children may initially object to your line of questioning, so you will need to help them understand the purposes behind it.

As a parent, it is much better for you to discover any misbehaviors of your child than to find them out from a bishop, mission president, or therapist. In fact, the serpent in you may sound a lot like your conscience at this point, nagging you to have that difficult interview with your child that you have been avoiding. Polls show that youth throughout the world are struggling with importance of God, church attendance, and prayer.[6] Parents often have the wisdom of the serpent, but they must also have the serpent's courage to impart that wisdom to their loved ones.

Once hard questions have been asked, hard choices must be made. The dove part of you will encourage you to pray and fast for your children, as well you should. Again, I don't wish to take anything away from the promptings of the dove. However, prayer is a much easier chore than following the promptings of the serpent. Before his mission, does your son require counseling for anxiety, depression, or social insecurity? Missionaries are expected to open their mouths and boldly profess the gospel. Can your son do that? Is your daughter prepared to enter the temple for the first time, secure in knowing what to expect there and the symbolism behind each step?

The world is trying to beat down its righteous youth through social media and other temptations. False doctrine is very likely leaking into your home, despite your best efforts. The dove inside you will persuade you to have faith that God will help you sort out your family problems. The serpent side of you will encourage you to be proactive with your children, ask the difficult questions, and make the difficult choices. Do both.

I can say little more about allowing the serpent side of the gospel to influence how you raise your family or run a home. This book is not meant to be a discussion on how to raise children. It's meant to remind Latter-day Saints that they have to be willing to think like a serpent sometimes. The scriptures prove that being Christlike does *not* mean to always be dovelike. All is not well in Zion.

Few Church members actually want to be wise like the serpent. It requires one to be bluntly honest and willing to discuss unrighteous behavior that may be both embarrassing and disappointing. It may require honest assessments of your children's mental stability, emotional challenges, or social insecurities. In Church lessons, we are taught to be faithful, prayerful, and dovelike. And we should be. But we shouldn't think that faith and prayer will be enough.

Problems in today's world also require practical, serpentlike solutions to defend our homes and church. The solutions of the past, and the naiveté of the dove, do not work anymore.

Chapter 3

The Wisdom of the Serpent in Defending our Religious Beliefs

THE TEMPTATIONS THAT LEAK INTO OUR HOMES TODAY HAVE CHANGED little from earlier in the century, though the internet has given pornography a new vehicle for wider distribution. Social media has also given critics of the Latter-day Saint religion new opportunities to spread misinformation about the Church.

For some reason, the Church comes under a lot of attack from the outside world. It is a unique religion and draws attention without even trying. Members believe that the Church is led by a prophet and other inspired leaders, a claim that triggers alarms in many people. Indeed, there have been numerous false prophets in recent history, such as Jim Jones, David Koresh, and Marshall Applewhite. Church critics assume that Latter-day Saint prophets must be frauds as well. They point to warnings about false prophets given in the Bible. In Matthew 7:15, the Savior warns everyone,

> Beware of false prophets, which come to you in sheep's clothing, but inwardly they are ravening wolves.

On a side note, from this verse many critics conclude that present-day prophets are false and approach you in disguise. This is a good example of how critics can mislead with faulty interpretations of a scripture, an approach that will be discussed in later chapters. Logically, however, since Jesus Christ warned us about false prophets, doesn't that imply that there must be *true* prophets as well? If all prophets were false, wouldn't the Savior have made that fact clear, warning us to disbelieve *anyone* claiming to be a prophet? By warning us to beware of false prophets, the Savior declares you must sort out the ravening wolves from the true prophets. The caution only makes sense if both true and false prophets exist. As with this example, the next several chapters are dedicated to pointing out the myriad of logic breakdowns found in criticisms and attacks on The Church of Jesus Christ of Latter-day Saints. I will not be making deep doctrinal arguments. A serpentlike discovery of blatant falsehoods and faulty assumptions will suffice.

When someone attacks Church doctrine, we must first determine if the attack is upon the existence of God, the truth of Christian religions in general, or a specific attack upon The Church of Jesus Christ of Latter-day Saints. Defending the existence of God or the Atonement of Jesus Christ requires a whole different set of arguments than defending the doctrine of the restored church. Most critics don't want to risk offending Christians by attacking Christianity. The Latter-day Saints are a much smaller group, so we are a much easier target.

Many anti-Mormon writings, blogs, Facebook groups, and videos are produced by disenchanted members who have left the Church and, in their anger, turn against it. This obsession has been going on since the Church was founded. A young man named Ezra Booth joined the Church in May of 1831 and was called to serve a mission the very next month (D&C 52:23). But by September, Booth renounced the Church in a very public fashion, writing nine critical letters that were printed in the *Ohio Star* newspaper.[7] This may have been the first published anti- Mormon literature ever written. Another convert and leader in the Church, William McLellin, was baptized in August of 1831 and was called to the Quorum of the Twelve Apostles in February 1835.

Despite the personal revelations and church callings he received, McLellin's apostasy grew and he was excommunicated in 1838. Rather than just walk away from the Church, McLellin joined the Missouri mobs to forcibly drive the Church out of the state. He asked the sheriff holding Joseph Smith if he could publicly flog the prophet. If he lived today, one might expect that McLellin would have started up his own anti-Mormon podcast.

Over the decades that the Church enjoyed unprecedented growth, anti-Mormon literature was published and distributed by religions that feared losing their membership to the Latter-day Saint faith. People were warned to send away the white-shirted missionaries if they came knocking at their door. When I was investigating The Church of Jesus Christ of Latter-day Saints as a freshman in college, I let an uncle of mine know about my study. This uncle was a born-again Christian and a deeply religious man. Since my immediate family had drifted away from church attendance of any kind, I thought he would be pleased. Instead, my uncle sent me a manila envelope stuffed with anti-Mormon literature. I presented the collection of pamphlets to the missionaries who were teaching me and asked them to explain it. They handled the situation well. They did not try to answer every attack, but assured me, as I would learn in later years, that these questions had already been answered many times.

Today, attacks against the Church continue, but the format has changed. Instead of pamphlets, there are now websites, blogs, Facebook discussion groups, and podcasts dedicated to criticizing the Church and encouraging members to leave it. In what seems to be a strategic maneuver, many anti-Mormon podcasts and social groups have innocuous titles one would expect from pro- Mormon sites. I once joined a Facebook group which invited Latter-day Saint members to join a Bible discussion group. I thought the group would be a good forum to discuss gospel doctrine between Church members and non-members. It wasn't. There was an ongoing barrage of attacks upon the Church, often thinly veiled as questions. Comments always had deep veins of sarcasm and disbelief running through them. Though a few missionary-minded Saints gamely tried to address the raised issues, it became apparent that no one in the discussion group was sincerely seeking knowledge.

The word "argument" has two definitions. An argument can be a dispute, such as in the statement, "My spouse and I had a bad argument." Such verbal fights tend to be very emotional and damaging. I don't recommend them. However, an argument can also be "a set of reasons or evidence in support of a conclusion," such as in, "You make a good argument."[8] We are instructed in the Church to *not* dispute with anyone, even critics of the Church. Dispute creates dissension and discord. Therefore, this book will *not* give you instruction on how to take the offensive in a religious argument and win it. However, this book *will* suggest how you can defend the Church and its doctrine when it is criticized. A righteous nation is allowed to defend itself in battle. Likewise, faithful Church members are allowed to defend themselves against attacks on their religion. Please note that the main purpose in defining these defenses is for you, the reader. I hope these arguments strengthen your self-defenses so that you are not carried away by the conclusions of our critics. So armed, you can then help those you love to understand the flaws of criticisms against your faith. This battle with Church critics has occurred since the days of the New Testament. As Paul pled with the Ephesians,

> That we henceforth be no more children, tossed to and fro, and carried about with every wind of doctrine, by the sleight of men,

> and cunning craftiness, whereby they lie in wait to deceive. (Ephesians 4:14)

If we do not want to be "carried about with every wind of doctrine," members of The Church of Jesus Christ of Latter-day Saints should be familiar with the responses to criticisms of their religion.

It is unknown how much the plethora of anti-Mormon websites, podcasts, and blogs are actually affecting church activity. Church attendance has decreased within all Christian churches over the past couple of decades and it is impossible to identify and sort out all the causes. However, I have heard many of my fellow Latter-day Saints lament about how their families have been negatively affected by one social media or another. There are so many websites, videos, and podcasts that exist for the sole purpose of criticizing the Church. One would expect there to be some damage to testimonies, especially of those who spend more of their time reading, viewing, or listening to social media.

Undoubtedly, there are hundreds of reasons why people abandon their religion. There is little this book can say to dissuade those who have left their religion for purely emotional reasons. Emotion does not care about logic, facts, or truths. However, for those Saints who have left or are considering leaving their religion due to an intellectual disagreement with a doctrine or an event in Church history, then I encourage you to read on.

There is so much misinformation published and in podcasts about The Church of Jesus Christ of Latter-day Saints. There are no indications that the media will become more sympathetic to the Church. At the time of writing this book, a new television series called Under the Banner of Heaven has just premiered. It makes the Church out to be cultish and domineering, a faulty depiction we have seen before. I don't want to give the show any more attention than it has drawn already. Since I was writing this book, I was more interested in how the show was being received than in the show itself. Reviews were mixed, though polarized. Some reviewers defended the Latter-day Saint faith, but others seemed to like the show because it cast the religion in the bad light they thought it deserved.[9]

As mentioned earlier, The Church of Jesus Christ of Latter-day Saints continues to draw public attention. In an increasingly unreligious world, an active religion like the Latter-day Saint faith is bound to attract negative media portrayals—and viewership. This television series is just the latest disparagement in a continuing saga. To repeat, this book was *not* written to encourage you to go out looking for fights with Church critics. The purpose of this book is to prepare you to recognize the strategies and intents behind the criticisms and attacks upon Latter-day Saint doctrine and history. Many such "questions" are crafted only to damage your testimony of the Church. This book can't prepare you with the specific answer to every complaint and criticism of the Church. However, it can prepare you to recognize the faulty foundations on which such questions are based. The following chapters will encourage you to develop the wisdom of the serpent. To successfully do that, you need to be able to recognize how critics of the Church deceive and how those attacks can be unraveled.

Chapter 4

The State of Religious Debate

GENERALLY, WHEN WE PICK UP A BOOK ABOUT LATTER-DAY SAINT doctrine, we expect that it will give us the answers to the questions that are directed at the Church. Indeed, there are many well-written books available that go into detail about Church history and doctrine. Latter-day Saints should have a passing knowledge of Church doctrine, its history, the scriptures, and theology.

If you have a friend who is sincerely curious about Latter-day Saint doctrine, knowing and communicating the answers is all you really need to do. However, we live in a world where few questions asked about the Church are genuine. Often, such questions mask an attack or criticism of the Church and its doctrine. Questions can make unsupported claims sound real. They can incorporate assumptions that are patently untrue. Questions that have been fully answered can be reworded and repeated. It is difficult for Church members to always be prepared for such questions. This is what Church critics hope for—to surprise, to instill doubt, and then to weaken testimonies. So, besides being prepared to *answer* gospel questions, we should first be prepared to *question* the questions.

It is sometimes difficult to separate a seeker of truth from a seeker of dissension. Church members want to be good missionaries. When someone asks a question about the Latter-day Saint religion, we should try our best to answer it. We hope that everyone is trying to learn the truth. However, we must also realize that we are living in a world where honest inquiries about religion are rather rare. Many questions are asked to confuse and instill doubt in those who try to answer them. Such questions range from subtle pokes at a religious belief to a series of questions designed to undermine the testimony of faithful Church members.

There are a host of unfair questions and criticisms of the Church out there, often presented by anti-Mormon podcast hosts, bloggers, YouTubers, and writers. Knowing the untruths and assumptions behind such attacks may help you personally, or it may help you explain them to a family member or friend. How can a simple question be designed to be an attack? Let's consider a few such questions, as examples.

"Did you know that Joseph Smith stole the Book of Mormon stories from a fictional manuscript written by Solomon Spaulding?" This question does not ask you if the accusation that Joseph Smith plagiarized the Book of Mormon is true. The questioner *assumes* the accusation is true and simply wants to confirm that you were aware of it. This question is worded to infuse doubt and confusion and put you on the defensive about Church history.

In religious discussions, simple "yes-no" questions can be dangerous. They are rather like the question, "Are you still cheating on your spouse?" The question offensively assumes that you have been cheating on your spouse, and the questioner is curious if you are still doing so. By answering "Yes" or "No" you essentially admit that their assumption is true. Only by pointing out the inherent fallacy of that assumption can you defend your honor. Thus, only an answer such as, "I have never cheated on my spouse," will deter argument.

Rhetorical questions are questions that are asked without expecting an answer. There is no real inquiry in them. For example, someone might ask you, "How can Mormons believe in polygamy?" Since you don't know how all Mormons came to their beliefs, there is no answer to such a question. You could launch into a complex explanation, requiring reviews of Church history, references to the Old Testament, and explanations of when polygamy is needed and when it is not. However, it may be better to ask your interrogator to clarify their question. Take heed that rhetorical questions like this one are often designed to make a negative statement and cast doubt on the subject matter, not to actually gather information.

Debates Are No Longer Debates

There are few formal religious debates anymore. Doctrinal debates with a moderator, microphones, and time limits on responses are no longer popular. However, please know that informal religious debates are occurring every day. Anti-Mormon podcasts, blogs, Facebook groups, and websites are readily available on your phone, tablet, or laptop at any time.

In the days of formal debates, it was common practice for one debate team to take a question from the opposing team and tear it to shreds before trying to answer it. What are the assumptions behind that question? What are your references? Is the question even answerable? Are you asking for speculation? Questions in a debate are not designed to gather knowledge.

They are designed to distract and lead the discussion in a particular direction. Debate teams are trained to resist allowing their debate to drift off in unwanted directions.

Formal debates are still found in the political arena. Is our economy strong? Is our foreign policy with China effective? Who should be the next president of the United States? Compared to religious debate, however, political debate is simple. A political debate focuses only on the interaction of citizens and their government. We all understand what our government is. It has an organization. Its processes and laws are documented. Though political issues may be complex, they are limited in their scope to . . . well, politics.

Religious debate is much too broad of a discussion topic to allow such simplicity. In religious debate, one person may be an atheist while another believes she sees miracles from God every day. In a religious discussion, you can have faithful church members who believe God wants them to live pious, soft-spoken lives and others who party hard every weekend. Religious debates include *all* aspects of life, including religious observance, marriage, family, charity, foreign policy, and the reasons for earth life. Metaphorically speaking, political debates are narrow walkways between two buildings, while religious debates are six-lane highways with open fields on both sides.

Formal political debates are generally run by a neutral moderator, who makes sure the debaters follow rules of order and do not run over their allotted time. There is no such oversight or discipline in present-day debates about religion. In podcasts, videos, blogs, and social media, anyone can say anything. There is no penalty for being inaccurate, illogical, or spiteful. Half- truths are very popular, as it is always easier to convince someone about a falsehood with a little truth mixed in. Exaggeration, hyper-emotional responses to simple statements, sarcasm, and the use of lots of quote marks or air-quotes (e.g., Joseph Smith, a "prophet" of God) are very popular in such debates. Even when fully answered, the same attacks against the Latter-day Saint faith are repeated over and over again. Many of the criticisms I hear today were included in my uncle's anti-Mormon pamphlets that he sent me before my baptism, now over 40 years ago.

A reader, listener, or viewer must understand the enormous "spin" that an author can put on historical facts. Though you may hear the saying, "Let the facts speak for themselves," author and Church historian Keith Erekson denies the possibility.

> Facts don't speak, but storytellers do; therefore, it is essential to understand how interpretation happens, why storytellers speak the way they do, and how their stories work.[10]

Storytellers tell their stories in a way that advances their own agenda, perspective, or interpretation of history. Let me give you an example of how a history may be told. Please know that I tell this story only to make my point.

> This man was in trouble with the law from his very beginning. Shortly after his birth, his parents became fugitives from the law, and they had to flee the country to avoid arrest. After the arrest warrants had expired, the small family was able to return to their hometown. As a youth, this man fled from his parents while at a celebration in Jerusalem. Until he was about thirty years old, this man remained at home, doing rough labor. He never married. He started roaming the country, managing to collect a following of other vagabonds. He instructed His followers to turn away from their family religions. He associated with prostitutes, beggars, and lawyers. His teachings grew more popular and incited riots in Nazareth and Jerusalem. When one of His own followers betrayed him, church and state officials were finally able to arrest the man. He was tried for his crimes. Multiple witnesses gave testimony of his slander and claims of kingship. He was found guilty of conspiracy and treason against the state, and he was put to death for those crimes.

Sounds like a real scoundrel, doesn't he? I am, of course, giving a summary of the life of the Savior. Please note that all the statements in my biography are accurate. They are just written with a particular purpose in mind. You may have been thinking, "But you're not telling the whole story!" Well of course I'm not; few people ever do. The point is—a decent writer can make anyone sound like a felon. Have you read anti-Mormon literature about Joseph Smith? Do you really think it was a fair and unbiased assessment of Joseph's life?

In this book, I am not going to try to list all the accusations that critics have made of Latter-day Saint doctrine and history. That would be a very long book indeed. I am not going to try to give you all the possible responses to those attacks either, as that would be an even longer book.

However, there are similarities in the *strategies* behind those accusations that I would hope you can identify from reading this book. If you are a Church member who is frequenting anti- Mormon websites to find the truth about Joseph Smith, you might want to be aware of the tactics being used to sway your opinion. Or, if you want to be able to respond to friends and family who are listening to podcast interviews of angry people who left the Church, you should also be aware of the strategies of those podcast hosts. Let's start this review with the good old days, when people read books and other printed media to learn about their world.

Anti-Mormon Books

Attacks on the Church have been going on for a long time. Most of the anti-Mormon pamphlets and books were published before the year 2000, when we turned to the internet as our favored medium of communication. In the 1900s, the Church had enjoyed significant growth.

Missionaries were being sent all over the world and finding success. For leaders of other religions, The Church of Jesus Christ of Latter-day Saints was a threat. Thus, the Church came under an ongoing siege of criticisms and negative literature.

One of the more well-known books of the past century was *They Lie in Wait to Deceive*, by Robert and Rosemary Brown, published in January 1950. Then we had *No Man Knows My History: The Life of Joseph Smith*, written by Fawn M. Brodie (a niece of David O. McKay) and published in August 1995. *The God Makers*, written by Ed Decker and Dave Hunt, was published in 1997 and caused some stir. More recently, *Letter to a CES Director*, a PDF booklet written by Jeremy T. Runnells and published in April 2013 once again repeated these same old charges against the Church. Its tone is aggressive and accusatory. It is written as if the questions were all newly discovered cover-ups by the Church. Nothing could be further from the truth.

Michael R. Ash gives his response to those charges in his book called *Bamboozled by the "CES Letter.*[11] The book is highly informative and entertaining.

As happens with printed publications, the popularity of each book attacking the Church came and went. By comparison, those were easier days for the defenders of Latter-day Saint doctrine. Writing a book is an extensive process and the author must find someone to agree to publish it. Only a few people were willing to dedicate that amount of effort. However, today it is very easy and inexpensive to set up a website, a blog, or a podcast. There are currently over two million podcasts available for your listening pleasure.[12] A surprising number of those podcasts are aimed at criticizing the Church. Unlike dealing with books that come out every couple of years, today's attack is continual.

Anti-Mormon Blogs

According to one report, there were more than 500 million blogs on the internet.[13] There are blogs about every sport and pastime. There are fan club blogs that discuss the activities and relationships of famous movie stars. Pick any subject and there is bound to be at least one blog to discuss it.

There are certain people who, as long as they can remain anonymous, feel they can write awful things to total strangers with whom they disagree. Such people love blogs of course. When blogs were first attached to news articles, I volunteered to find online articles about the Church and add relevant and positive answers to any questions in the blog that was attached to the article. I found that I couldn't do it. Earlier blog entries, to which I was being asked to respond, were too virulent, snarky, and profane. I got so angry with them that a spiritual, calm response became impossible for me. Sadly, people can become stuck in the mire of such blogs.

Anti-Mormon Podcasts

I have hosted a pro-Mormon podcast of my own over the past two years. In the midst of researching other Latter-day Saint podcasts, I found that many of the internet results for the keywords "Latter-day Saint Podcast" were anti-Mormon. As mentioned earlier, many of these podcasts are innocuously titled, making them good examples of "wolves in sheep's clothing." Church members can be lured into thinking they are listening to a podcast that is teaching positive Church doctrine, but then gradually realize it is not positive at all.

At first, I marveled at the fact that people could be so angry with the Church that they would spend hours each week listening to podcasts of other people being angry with the Church. Neil A. Maxwell also expressed his dismay in a talk comparing ex-member critics of the Church to tares.

> Some real tares even masquerade as wheat, including the few eager individuals who lecture the rest of us about Church doctrines in which they no longer believe. They criticize the use of Church resources to which they no longer contribute. They condescendingly seek to counsel the Brethren whom they no longer sustain. Confrontive, except of themselves, of course, they leave the Church, but they cannot leave the Church alone.[14]

In listening to present-day anti-Mormon podcasts, you will hear relatively few discussions on theology or philosophy. However, you will hear a lot of snarky comments. To be snarky means to be critical, derisive, and sarcastic. It is the best adjective I can find to describe the comments I hear on anti-Mormon podcasts. Many such podcasts often start their episodes with a review of the week's news about the Church. If you've ever watched a late-night talk show monologue, you know that anyone can take a news report and make snarky comments about it. However, it is not a fair forum for discussion. These podcast hosts can make outrageous statements, without anyone there to point out poor assumptions and logical fallacies.

The main program of many anti-Mormon podcasts consists of interviews with ex-members. Usually, they have been offended by a bishop, stake leader, or other ward member for doing something insensitive. They identify The Church of Jesus Christ of Latter-day Saints as being responsible for this offense, because it was caused by one of its members. The lack of logic behind this rationale should be rather obvious. Yet almost every week anti-Mormon podcasts are able to find angry Latter-day Saint members or ex-members to be on their show. On the other hand, statistically speaking, this should not be a surprise.

Where Do Anti-Mormon Podcasts Find Their Guests?

I am a convert to the Latter-day Saint religion. During the first nineteen years of my life, I attended church services of several Protestant religions. In those faiths, I observed that most members attend Sunday services, listen to their minister's sermon, and then go home. Further interaction with other church members is not really required. This is generally not true in The Church of Jesus Christ of Latter-day Saints. You may be a "Sunday attendee only" member if you wish, but you will be encouraged to serve in a calling. The bishop must call presidents, counselors, teachers, advisors, and activity planners for all the supporting organizations in the ward—Primary, Young Women, Young Men, Relief Society, elders quorum, missionary committee, activities committee, etc. Not only on Sunday, but throughout the whole week, all those people interact with one another. Assignments are given, directives are communicated, and updates are reported via text, phone call, email, or website entry. Depending on your calling, you may have dozens of interactions with other Church members in any given week. Within the whole ward, there will be hundreds of such interactions from one Sunday to the next.

With all of those interactions, is it a surprise that Latter-day Saint members offend one another on occasion? If you know human beings at all, you know that interactions sometimes generate conflict. It is hard to compare The Church of Jesus Christ of Latter-day Saints to other churches where the only interaction one might have with another member is waving at a familiar face in the parking lot.

One can compare a Latter-day Saint ward to a rock tumbler. As they carry out their callings, Church members interact with one other, rather like rocks interact in a rock tumbler. Occasionally, disagreements occur, and two rocks collide, knocking off some sharp edges. Such collisions are painful, often causing hurt feelings for a while. But the offended members purposefully work on forgiving one another, as taught in the scriptures. They gradually get past their anger and start to socialize again. Learning to get along with other people is one of the most important lessons of Earth life. At the end of the day, you have a handful of polished, smoothed rocks, or, dropping the metaphor, a ward full of people experienced in serving together, forgiving one another, and getting along.

At least . . . that is the way it is *supposed* to work in the Church. With easy access to various social media outlets, some Church members get so angry that they take their grievances online, either in a podcast, blog, or YouTube. Generally, this public disclosure seems to cement the grievance in place for those offended and only rarely do they find their way back. Such losses are sad and disappointing for everyone in the Church. However, the Church must continue to call members to responsibilities that require frequent interactions with others. We need those opportunities to learn how to deal with, love, and forgive our brothers and sisters—however obnoxious they (or we) may be.

Attacks Are Personal

Though anti-Mormon podcasters will specifically name leaders in the Church whom they are criticizing with harsh and sarcastic words, they will often end such reports pointing out that their criticisms are directed at the *organization* of the Church, not the individual. Apparently, they don't want their less dedicated listeners to feel guilty about all the bad-mouthing that is going on. Yet, I must ask, "Which part of the organization of the Church is so insulting?" Are the physical assets of the Church, like the Church Office Building, causing a problem? Probably not. Like all corporations, institutions, and religions, the Church organization is made up of *people.*

So, who in the Church makes up the "organization" being criticized? The First Presidency? The Quorum of Apostles? All the people who work in the Church Office Building? Who are these tactless, awful Church members who are abusing other members in so many ways? It's easy to blame a faceless, nameless entity like the "Church organization" for evils and offenses. But the harsh criticisms, sarcasm, and snarky rebukes are directed at people, no matter how much the anti-Mormon podcasts may claim otherwise.

Trashing a person's reputation on social media and then saying, "Nothing personal," is deceptive. Church leaders who are attacked generally stay out of the fray, perhaps seeing it as part of the job of doing good and helping their fellow man.

The Strong Testimonies of Anti-Mormon Podcasters and Bloggers

In the end, I have to give some credit to the hosts of anti-Mormon podcasts. Their testimonies that the Church is false are *much* stronger than my testimony that the Church is true. In any decision I make, I always ask myself the question, "What if I'm wrong?". How harsh are the consequences of making a poor choice in this decision? Can I return my purchase if I don't like it?

If my choice to be a faithful member of the Latter-day Saint faith is wrong . . . I still don't believe that my Final Judgment will be too bad. I gave my time and tithing to the Church. I tried to keep the Sabbath day holy, pray daily, and be honest in my dealings. If I am wrong and the Church is false, well, the Lord will probably chide me for making a poor choice of religions on which to base my worship. Yet, I was still faithful in keeping His commandments and trying to help others. So, I truly believe I will be okay in the Judgment, despite what might have been a poor selection of religion.

However, if the anti-Mormon podcasters are wrong and The Church of Jesus Christ of Latter-day Saints *is* the true church of Jesus Christ, I don't believe that the Final Judgment will go well for them. I think Jesus Christ meant it when He said,

> And whoso shall receive one such little child in my name receiveth me.
>
> But whoso shall *offend one of these little ones which believe in me*, it were better for him that a millstone were hanged about his neck, and that he were drowned in the depth of the sea. (Matthew 18:5–6, italics added)

This verse has always struck me as being surprisingly violent. This is an unveiled truth against those who would turn His children against Him. I believe that bloggers, podcasters, or videographers who encourage Church members to stop attending services and remove themselves from the Church fall well within the definition of offending the Savior's little ones. So, anti-Mormon broadcasters must have a strong testimony in their negative judgment of the Church. The penalties for being wrong in that judgment sound very serious indeed.

The state of religious debate today is rarely respectful or designed to educate listeners. It is designed to offend and dissuade those who can be entrapped by false information. As members of The Church of Jesus Christ of Latter-day Saints, we need to take the warnings of the Savior to "be ye therefore wise as serpents" (Matthew 10:16) and to "beware of false prophets" (Matthew 7:15) more seriously. We need to be willing and faithful enough to understand the answers to present-day attacks on the Church. Many of these questions are complex and may require some research, but the Church has many resources. The arsenal of anti-Mormon criticisms is actually rather limited. If you can recognize the lack of reason behind each smear, you will be better prepared to defend both your own testimony and those of your loved ones.

Before we start an assessment of anti-Mormon criticisms, I would like to take a chapter and consider how we got where we are today. As mentioned, the Latter-day Saint religion has not really changed its history or doctrine over the past century, so the criticisms and condemnations have not really changed much either. What is different today? What has changed in our society that has allowed these old verbal assaults to convince our young adult generations to leave the Church?

Chapter 5

Living in a Day of Emotion over Reason

Near the end of 2019, we first heard about COVID-19, otherwise known as the coronavirus pandemic. Worldwide, people were told to stay in their homes. Stores and restaurants closed their doors. By September the death toll had reached 200,000 in the United States.[15] About one year later, the long-awaited COVID-19 vaccine was made available in clinics and the pharmacies at our local grocery stores. By April 2021, over 200 million vaccine shots had been administered. Strangely . . . unexpectedly . . . millions of vaccines remained in their vials. After a year of quarantines and inconvenience, millions of people refused to be vaccinated against COVID-19. As of this writing, only 68% of the nation's population has been fully vaccinated.[16] My son-in-law Chris, who studied the matter, explained it to me, "The technical data has proven that the vaccine is safe. But we live in a day and age when *no one trusts anyone*."

Today we hear debates about the definition of gender. For millennia, mankind has followed the biological definition of gender. Today it is a matter of emotional debate and legislation.

We hear debates about the need for law enforcement, an aspect of government that has been recognized by every advanced civilization throughout the history of the world. Several cities in the country defunded their police departments. Racial tensions are running extremely high.

Political debates are more emotional.

Anyone who has had an overly emotional argument with their spouse realizes that such disputes rarely resolve anything. When emotions are running high, it is nearly impossible to negotiate a compromise. We stop trying to understand our antagonist's point of view. Relationships are damaged. It is not surprising that the scriptures recommend that we learn to quell our emotions when dealing with others. In the first chapter of James we read,

> Wherefore, my beloved brethren, let every man be swift to hear, slow to speak, slow to wrath:
>
> For the wrath of man worketh not the righteousness of God. (James 1:19–20)

As might be expected, the books of Psalms and Proverbs contain similar recommendations.

> He that is slow to wrath is of great understanding: but he that is hasty of spirit exalteth folly. (Proverbs 14:29)

> A soft answer turneth away wrath: but grievous words stir up anger. (Proverbs 15:1)

We live in a time when many of our communications come through social media posts. However, social media posts cannot be very long. Media outlets often restrict word counts and few people have the patience to read long posts anyway. Thus limited, one simply doesn't have the time to build strong, logical cases for an argument. Consequently, posts must jump straight to their conclusions, which are often quite emotional. The anonymity of social media allows its users to rant, rave, curse, and offend. Social media sites now strongly warn users to curb their aggression—and regularly remove posts of those who don't.

Using profanity has always been considered an expression of extreme emotion. A profane word was thought to be a release of anger or surprise. In a society based on emotion over reason, we are seeing an increase in the profanity in public discourse, television shows and literature. We have become so emotional as a country that we no longer attempt to curb our profanity. As pointed out by a *Time* article entitled, "The Rudeness Epidemic,"

> Some researchers point to the increase in crude public discourse, both from political leaders and in online discussion—which encourages outsized emotions—as the gateway rudeness that has led to the current wave.[17]

Emotion has replaced reason as our go-to response to life. Airlines report an alarming increase of verbal and physical abuse toward their flight attendants.[18] Women who go emotionally ballistic in stores or restaurants when they don't get their way have become so common that they have been given their own name—Karen.

We have all heard about the development of a new "cancel culture." Those who make comments that are deemed racially or otherwise offensive are publicly shamed over social media. Indeed, rude commenters should be ashamed. However, today's cancel culture has become ultra-sensitive, looking for offense where none was ever intended. People are even trying to cancel comments that are not opinions, but provable facts. How can we have discussions about solving issues in our country if the truths of our problems are cancelled and not voiced? How do we learn from our history, if we scrub our past of the imprudent words and actions of irresponsible but well-known persons? In a 1948 speech to the British House of Commons, Winston Churchill said, "Those that fail to learn from history are doomed to repeat it."[19] Can we not view our history as a record of mankind's successes and failures, and learn from them? The idea of scrubbing our history books demonstrates a new high in emotional extremism, to the detriment of logic, reason, and learning.

The Reason-Hope-Faith-Testimony Cycle

This increase in emotional response to challenges in life also affects the Latter-day Saint community. One's temporal life often has unsettling effects on one's spiritual life. One's testimony, much like our political beliefs and other philosophies, is built on a foundation of reason. I propose, in fact, that testimonies begin with reason, which is followed by hope, then by faith, and then by testimony.

Let's start with Reason. Church services are filled with talks and lessons that logically examine each of our doctrines. In the scriptures, the Lord continually invites us to reason together.

In Doctrine and Covenants 50:10–12, we read,

> And now come, saith the Lord, by the Spirit, unto the elders of his church, and let us reason together, that ye may understand;
>
> Let us reason even as a man reasoneth one with another face to face.
>
> Now, when a man reasoneth he is understood of man, because he reasoneth as a man; even so will I, the Lord, reason with you that you may understand.

The Lord uses the word "reason" or "reasoneth" six times in this short scriptural reference. God has been reasoning with His children for a long time. In Doctrine and Covenants, section 45, we read,

> Wherefore, come ye unto it, and with him that cometh I will reason *as with men in days of old*, and I will show unto you my strong reasoning. (D&C 45:10, italics added)

We attend school to read books and listen to lectures to understand the reasons the earth was created and why we were born here. We gradually accumulate knowledge. Once we realize that a doctrine is reasonable, Hope starts to dawn that it is true. We come to understand the need for God and dare to hope for the promise of eternal life. Is God actually our Heavenly Father who loves us? I hope that is true. Is there life after death? I really hope that is true too. We ponder and pray about those hopes. We move from the mental task of study and reasoning to the emotion of hope. But our mental conclusion that these teachings could be true must precede our prayers. If we initiate a prayer without hope, we should probably not expect a confirmatory answer.

Through more study and prayers, we collect evidence. As a result of living a gospel-centered life, we feel happier and more optimistic. We gradually develop faith that gospel principles are true. Faith is an interesting, somewhat complex combination of knowledge and emotion. To support this claim, I must quote for you the classic go-to verse on faith found in Alma 32:21.

> And now as I said concerning faith—faith is not to have a perfect knowledge of things; therefore if ye have faith ye hope for things which are not seen, which are true.

This verse teaches two principles. First, faith is not to have a perfect knowledge, but it does *start* with imperfect or incomplete knowledge. That knowledge is worked into the foundation of logic and reason that supports our faith and hope. Secondly, faith is a hope for things which are not yet seen. This makes faith both an emotional conclusion as well as a logical one.

To recap, reason and understanding raise hope. Hope blooms into faith. Faith then develops into testimony. Testimony is really just a statement of our faith—meaning it is a blend of our reasoned knowledge and our emotions of hope and faith. We bear our testimonies, probably using the words "I know" more than we should. Testimonies are part knowledge and part emotion. They cannot be conclusively proven. Since we must live by faith, testimonies were never meant to be verified, in this life at least.

As Church members, we should seek to be in a constant cycle of Reason, Hope, Faith, and Testimony. As the earlier quote by Dr. King concludes, we want to seek knowledge and understanding as we study the gospel. Then we can allow ourselves to hope for (and have faith in) what we have learned. However, this cycle of building reason and faith has been broken for many of our younger generations, as they allow their emotions to rule their lives. A perceived slight or a simple correction by a church leader becomes a monumental offense from which they can see no possible recovery. They leave their religion, justifying their actions on an emotional response to an unintended offense.

Tipping the Balance of Reason and Emotion

In his book *The Happiness Hypothesis*, author and social psychologist Jonathan Haidt constructed an analogy that will help us to understand the relationship between our reasoning mind and our emotions. He proposes that we think of our emotions as an elephant and our logical mind as being the rider of that elephant. The rider holds the reins and can direct the elephant to turn, stop, or go. But the rider can only influence the elephant when it has no desire to follow its own path. When the elephant wants to go its own way, the rider cannot stop it.

> In sum, the rider is an advisor or servant; not a king, president, or charioteer with a firm grip on the reins. The rider is . . . conscious, controlled thought. The elephant, in contrast, is everything else. The elephant includes the gut feelings, visceral reactions, emotions, and intuitions that comprise much of the automatic system. The elephant and the rider each have their own intelligence, and when they work together well they enable the unique brilliance of human beings. But they don't always work together well.[20]

My concern is that our younger generations have learned to allow the elephant of their emotions to dictate their response to religion and, often, life in general. As the elephant is stronger than its rider, emotions are stronger influencers than our reason. If allowed, emotions will shout down the arguments of the logical mind. Especially when we have had a rough time (such as during a long COVID quarantine), our emotions gather steam. Eventually they shout, as portrayed in the 1976 movie *Network*, "I'm mad as hell and I'm not going to take this anymore!"[21] When the target of that anger is the Church, reasoning is no longer heard, much less considered.

I included this chapter as a preface for the next chapters that offer logical arguments countering the attacks against The Church of Jesus Christ of Latter-day Saints. If my arguments encounter the raging emotional elephant of your anger and frustration, my reasoning is going to have a tough time getting through to you. I hope that my words are not being read over the roar of anger, sarcasm, bitterness, and resentment of an agitated emotional state. We seem to be dealing with such emotions on a global scale. However, for each of us personally, loss of emotional control and reasoning cannot be allowed to last. At some point, we need to start having rational discussions again; we need to let our reason regain control.

While emotional release may feel satisfying for a moment, it is our reason that should guide our understanding of the gospel and our decision to live it or not. We then open the door for our spiritual self to confirm those conclusions.

Chapter 6
Logical Fallacies

When I first joined The Church of Jesus Christ of Latter-day Saints, I announced my decision to my grandmother. She responded, "I knew a Mormon family in Florida. I remember they didn't have any curtains in their home. Aren't Mormons allowed to have curtains?" Her question was genuine and not meant to criticize. My grandmother had only met one family of Mormons, and that family didn't have curtains. Based on this anecdotal evidence, she extrapolated that Mormons weren't allowed to have curtains in their homes.

An anecdote is a short amusing story about a real incident or person. "Anecdotal evidence" is evidence that is based on one of these short stories. "Anecdotal fallacy" is when you try to take anecdotal evidence and form a conclusion around it.

From the website *Fallacy in Logic*, we read,

> In the world of advertising and marketing, *anecdotal evidence* is known as testimonials.
>
> The *anecdotal fallacy* is a logical fallacy that occurs when someone argues on the basis of anecdotal evidence. It's an extremely common type of error found in a wide variety of arguments. Moreover, it is often committed due to a lack of argumentation skills, however, it can be used intentionally as a debate tactic. . . .
>
> The fallacy of anecdotal evidence arises when someone uses proof that relies on personal testimonies, such as a story based on someone's individual experience, in order to support or refute a claim.[22]

Anecdotal evidence is not considered strong evidence because it is based on only one person's experience and opinion. However, both critics and faithful members of the Church quote anecdotal evidence abundantly.

When Church members bear their testimonies, they are presenting their own anecdotal evidence that The Church of Jesus Christ of Latter-day Saints is the true church of Jesus Christ. We can accept other people's anecdotal evidence, or we can develop our own anecdotes through spiritual experiences. Church members may argue that their testimony is made up of more than anecdotal evidence. However, over my career as an analytical chemist, I never encountered an instrument that could detect a spirit or spiritual communication. God cannot be analyzed, and heaven cannot be toured. So, although we recognize that anecdotal evidence is not the best evidence upon which to base our testimonies, it is all that we have available to us.

Anecdotal evidence is also used by critics of the Church. Anti-Mormon podcasts very commonly invite excommunicated or disenchanted ex-members onto their shows. These guests tell their story of how the Latter-day Saint church mistreated them in some way. This experience drove the podcast guest away from the Church. From such anecdotal evidence, the podcast usually comes to the conclusion that the Church is a manipulative, controlling organization that doesn't care about its members.

Does The Church of Jesus Christ of Latter-day Saints have bishops and stake presidents that can be rude, insensitive, and overly judgmental? Yes, it does. Does this prove that the Church is a manipulative, controlling organization that doesn't care about its members? Absolutely not.

There are millions of Latter-day Saints in the world. Some of them make mistakes. Others are offended at those mistakes or miscommunications. But there will never be enough anecdotal evidence to prove that insensitivity is a common trait within the Church.

Another fallacy in logic and reason, also taken from the website *Fallacy in Logic*, echoes another problem with anecdotal evidence.

> *Hasty generalization*, also known as "faulty generalization," is a logical fallacy in which someone generalizes from a too-small sample size. The conclusion of the argument is made hastily without looking at more reliable statistics which would enable the arguer to make a more accurate judgment about the situation or issue.[23]

According to the statistical report of the April 2022 General Conference, The Church of Jesus Christ of Latter-day Saints has 16,805,400 members.[24] Granted, thousands of people have left the Church. But if anti-Mormon podcasts have cycled 10,000 ex-members through their shows, that still only represents 0.06% of the population. That is the problem with anecdotal evidence and hasty generalization. Statistics and logic scream in pain at the conclusions drawn from them.

The testimonies of faithful Latter-day Saints that the Church *is* the true church of Jesus Christ are based on anecdotal evidence. The testimonies of ex-members that the Church is *not* the true church are *also* based on anecdotal evidence. One might think the two opinions cancel each other out. However, there is a very significant difference between the two conflicting testimonies. My positive testimony of The Church of Jesus Christ of Latter-day Saints is based on thousands of experiences. While it is still anecdotal evidence, that evidence spans over forty years of my adult life. The lost testimonies of angry ex-members are often based on a few bad interactions that may have occurred over just a few months. Thus, the levels of anecdotal evidence between the two sides really aren't comparable.

Perfecting the Saints

Many of the anecdotal stories that are given to leave the Church have to do with the misbehavior of its leadership and other members. Many discontented members seem to think that Church members should show elevated levels of love and concern for everyone. They believe that to be Christlike, Church members must always be dovelike, so must never reprove them or even disagree with them. This expectation is not often met in practice. The breadth of possible outcomes of human interactions is too great. I don't say this as an apology for how faithful Church members behave. One's serpentlike side must sometimes make appearances in the course of running a church ward. Some may claim that reprimands and counseling instruction are not part of a Christ-like attitude. In response to that accusation, I would like to once again quote Matthew 10:16–17, the scripture from which this book's title is taken. Jesus warned His apostles,

> Behold, I send you forth as sheep in the midst of wolves: be ye therefore wise as serpents, and harmless as doves.

Please note in this verse that the Savior compares people to *wolves*. Like the apostles of the early church, leaders must be aware that some people, including members, will take advantage of the organization. We don't like to recognize the necessity of such suspicion, but wariness is a needed attribute in our Church leaders. They must often think as serpents.

We find instruction on how Church leaders should act in Doctrine and Covenants, section 121. First, we read that ecclesiastical leaders need to have a dovelike attitude in dealing with others.

> No power or influence can or ought to be maintained by virtue of the priesthood, only by persuasion, by long-suffering, by gentleness and meekness, and by love unfeigned;
>
> By kindness, and pure knowledge, which shall greatly enlarge the soul without hypocrisy, and without guile— (D&C 121:41–42)

In the very next verse, the Lord gives instruction that Church leaders may need to apply their serpent side in dealing with others, but then show increased love afterwards.

> Reproving betimes with sharpness, when moved upon by the Holy Ghost; and then showing forth afterwards an increase of love toward him whom thou hast reproved, lest he esteem thee to be his enemy;
>
> That he may know that thy faithfulness is stronger than the cords of death. (D&C 121:43–44)

The Church of Jesus Christ is tasked with perfecting the saints—and it has a long way to go. Paul compares church members of his day to little children, who are "tossed to and fro, and carried about with every wind of doctrine, by the sleight of men, and cunning craftiness" (Ephesians 4:14). In other words, he tells us that Christians of the time were often gullible and were easily deceived. One must wonder if Paul would use similar wording to describe our membership today.

Complaints about Church members might also be addressed by remembering how very easy it is to join the Church. Converts do not have to fill out an application form. The Church doesn't run background checks or credit reports on those who wish to be baptized. In fact, we allow eighteen-year-old missionaries to decide if someone is worthy to be baptized. (Rather a scary thought if one thinks about it too long.) Since the Church does not screen new converts before they are allowed to join, should we expect members to be uncommonly kind and empathetic? Baptisms, though often very spiritual events, rarely change the basic personality of the new convert. We can only hope that years of Church activity will do that.

Indeed, we hope that attending church and being subject to the influence of the Holy Ghost will be a good influence on Church members. However, such a beneficial effect is not often readily apparent, and the Church doesn't make any claims that it is. Being offended by others is a consequence of living in an imperfect world with imperfect people. As Latter-day Saints, we understand quite well that there are no perfect people here.

Conflicts do occur. However, bishops and other leaders spend much time being concerned for their wards. It's a big part of their calling. If a conflict occurs, then there has been a breakdown of communication, or an expectation that, on the whole, Church members should be kinder and more sensitive than people who are not religious.

Generally speaking, I believe such an unintentional compliment to be true—but not so true as to avoid frequent exceptions to the rule. I have had my share of disagreements with other Church members, some of them rather intense. Fortunately, we resolved those conflicts, as we are taught in church to do. It sometimes took months to accomplish the task. Yet, such disagreements can be worked out. However, those who leave the Church over being offended never give themselves the opportunity to resolve their conflicts, so they will never know if it would have been possible.

Chapter 7

"The Church Should've Told Me"

In the past decade, The Church of Jesus Christ of Latter-day Saints has suffered declining attendance, along with all other religions.[25] The process for our younger adults leaving the Church almost always follows the same pattern. Many of our Latter-day Saint twenty-something adults learn some new doctrine or history about the Church that they didn't know before.[26] For some, it is a problem with the concept of polygamy. Others learned that Joseph Smith translated part of the Book of Mormon by looking at a seer stone in a hat. Disillusioned, these members accuse the Church of purposefully holding back historical realities from its members. They blame Church leaders for conspiring for over 150 years to keep secret any historical events that show the Church in a bad light. Their complaint in discovering such new facts is, "The Church should've told me!"

I have heard this complaint from young adult Church members who are very dear to me. I have studied criticisms of Latter-day Saint doctrine for years, so could calmly pummel each argument they made. But my responses did not change their minds. They came to their decision emotionally, not logically. In the end, they simply restated their decision. Despite my efforts, I couldn't change their emotional conclusions.

I would like to address this accusation that "The Church should've told me." Regarding this statement, I am not sure *when* the Church is supposed to tell its members about the deeper gospel principles and difficult-to-understand historical events in our history. I'm guessing that Primary presidents and parents throughout the Church would fight against teaching such doctrine to their children. They would be right in doing so. Children need to receive the milk of the gospel as children—and save the meat of the gospel until they are ready for it as adults (1 Corinthians 3:2).

However, an assessment of the critique, "The Church should've told me," reveals some gaps in logic when you stop to think about it. We need to do a serpentlike assessment of the declaration. If you have ever thought the Church was keeping anything from you, please consider the following five responses to the complaint.

#1—Church history information has always been available

My first argument against the complaint, "The Church should have told me," is that information on Church doctrine and history has always been available. I find accusations that the Church is hiding its history somewhat bewildering. Not surprisingly, the Church keeps its written history . . . in history books.

For example, many members leaving the Church claim that it has not been forthcoming in explaining the strange process Joseph used to translate the Book of Mormon. However, a description of the process Joseph Smith used to translate the Book of Mormon may be found in the readily available, six-volume *A Comprehensive History of The Church of Jesus Christ of Latter-day Saints*, written by B.H. Roberts. We read,

> He [Martin Harris] said that the Prophet possessed a Seer Stone, by which he was enabled to translate as well as with the Urim and Thummin, and for convenience he sometimes used the Seer Stone.
>
> At times when brother Joseph would attempt to translate he would look into the hat in which the stone was placed, [to exclude the light], he found he was spiritually blind and could not translate.[27]

The history book just referenced, *A Comprehensive History of The Church of Jesus Christ of Latter-day Saints,* is a six-volume history published in 1930 by B.H. Roberts. This set of books has been available for 92 years. *History of the Church of Jesus Christ of Latter-day Saints* is a seven-volume series (also edited by B.H. Roberts) that focuses on the prophet Joseph Smith. It was first published as a book in 1902. The *Latter-day Saint Biographical Encyclopedia* is a four-volume biographical series, written by Andrew Jensen and published between 1901 and 1936.

If the Church is trying to hide its history, it is doing a lousy job of it. With a little research, one can find any information desired on the translation of the Book of Mormon, history of polygamy, and the teachings of Brigham Young. Those who criticize that the Church doesn't reveal its history should perhaps check the Church history books.

#2—Church members do not attend church to debate controversial topics

Although many people live for controversy that they can debate over the internet, most Church members do not. Regular Church attendees usually attend church hoping for a break in dealing with the contentious outside world. The sweet and elderly Sister Jones does not want to thrash out how the practice of polygamy caused major issues in the early church. The father of six children who is working 60-hour weeks does not feel like debating what Brigham Young meant when he taught the Adam God theory. Church members want to find inspiration in church—not contention. They come to church to feel the Spirit, something that discussing sensitive, controversial subjects often does not usually allow.

Members do not view general conference to hear discussions about controversial subjects either. If the controversy is major, it may be discussed briefly. However, if general authorities tried to address every topic that someone considers questionable, they would have no time to talk about the subjects they think necessary for the Saints to hear. Controversial subjects are open to discussion of course, but usually in institute classes or more private settings with friends and family.

#3—Church members don't disparage God or His servants

It is pretty evident in the scriptures that God frowns on disparaging Him or His servants. The third commandment of the Ten Commandments is "Thou shalt not take the name of the Lord thy God in vain." This commandment is not just an injunction to avoid using profanity with the Lord's name. It means that God must be afforded the respect and obedience of His people. In a similar vein, God doesn't like His prophets to be criticized either.

In Numbers chapter 16, three men of the children of Israel, named Korah, Dathan, and Abiram, led a rebellion of 250 men against Moses. Apparently, they didn't like the way Moses and Aaron were leading the people. As these three men, their wives, and children stood in the door of their tents criticizing Moses, the earth simply swallowed them up. Then a fire consumed the 250 men who stood behind the tents in support of the rebellion. But it doesn't end there. The next day, the Israelites again congregated and were murmuring against Moses and Aaron, blaming them for the deaths of their rebellious friends. The Lord cursed them with a fast-acting plague that swept through the assembly. Moses had Aaron take incense as an atonement for the people and run into the crowd. His quick thinking worked. When the plague reached where Aaron stood, it stopped. But 14,700 murmurers died in that plague (Numbers 16:49). This event might be considered a definitive statement that the Lord objects to His servants being denounced.

The same warnings about criticizing Church leaders are found in latter-day revelations. In Doctrine and Covenants 28, we read,

> But, behold, verily, verily, I say unto thee, no one shall be appointed to receive commandments and revelations in this church excepting my servant Joseph Smith, Jun., for he receiveth them even as Moses. . . .
>
> And thou shalt not command him who is at thy head, and at the head of the church;
>
> For I have given him the keys of the mysteries, and the revelations which are sealed, until I shall appoint unto them another in his stead. (D&C 28:2, 6–7)

This tradition is so strong in the Latter-day Saint church that members don't disparage *any* of the servants of God mentioned in the scriptures. I was once teaching a gospel doctrine class about the prophet Elijah in the Old Testament. I read aloud the verses in the first chapter of 2 Kings where Elijah commanded fire to come down from the heavens and consume a hundred soldiers. These men had been ordered to get Elijah to come meet with their king and were just trying to do their jobs. I stated that Elijah seemed to have been a crusty old man and I didn't think I would have liked him much. I was immediately rebuked by an older sister in the class who told me I needed to study the scriptures until I did like him.

Obviously, there have been times in the history of the Church when its leaders made poor decisions. During the 1900s, our organization was unwilling to respond to questions about those decisions. To understand this reluctance, one must understand the generations who ran the Church over that period. For the Greatest Generation (born between 1910 to 1924) and the Silent Generation (born between 1925 to 1945), it is considered bad form to criticize religion or religious leaders.

My grandmother was aghast if family conversations turned a little risqué or critical of religion. She viewed any such talk as taking the Lord's name in vain.

Since Church members give respect to God's servants in the scriptures, it makes sense that latter- day Church leaders are not criticized either, whether they were leaders in 1830 or today. Even those men who first joined the restored church *and then left it* are not disparaged. Today we live in an age where every secret is known about anyone who spends time on social media. But this openness is only a recent cultural development. For centuries, most

Church members—both Latter-day Saint and non-Latter-day Saint—have refused to put their religious leaders in a bad light. Things have changed and our younger generations see only conspiracy in the Church's guarded descriptions of its history. However, this diplomacy can most simply be explained as a difference in social discourse between generations.

#4—Organizations don't disparage their history or founder

The Church has been criticized for "whitewashing" its history, which according to the Merriam-Webster dictionary, means "to gloss over or cover up."[28] Apparently, early Church leaders and writers should have been more honest in admitting their mistakes and poor decisions.

However, to such accusations I must ask, "Who in the history of mankind has *not* white-washed their history?" Every world empire, every government, every corporation, and every political leader wants their names to go down in history in the best possible light. Alexander the Great wasn't that great; in fact, he was a tyrant. Abraham Lincoln was actually a very unpopular president in his day. Honestly, how many Facebook profiles do you think are honest and unexaggerated?

Until the past few decades, when the public started to demand the dirt about its heroes, historians were loath to write about the mistakes and foibles of their chosen subjects. Why would anyone think that Church historians would be any different? Behind the criticism that the Church had not taught the mistakes of in its early founders is the assumption that other organizations *do* publicize their early poor decisions. The serpent within me would like to question that assumption. What organizations actually publicize the mistakes and goofs in their histories?

Very few religions, corporations, or other organizations record or publish the mistakes of their founders and early years. As a child, my family was Methodist, so I attended special catechism classes provided for the church's youth. John Wesley, who founded the Methodist Church, was never mentioned. I have never read criticisms by the Lutheran church of Martin Luther's rash actions in 1517. I have never heard Microsoft publicly question Bill Gates's actions when he started the company. Breakfast cereal companies Post and Kellogg's both had very . . . colorful founders. But don't expect to read those histories on the back of your cereal box any time soon. It is rare to hear calls for corporations, political parties, non-profit organizations, or other religions to broadly publicize their history. Those who call for greater transparency of Latter-day Saint church history may need to consider that such transparency is a new and rather rare trend.

Lastly, an organization will always be associated with its founder. It makes no sense for any organization to publicly question its founder's motives or actions, even if they occurred hundreds of years ago. Public relations departments try to avoid bad publicity—and criticizing the organization's founder means you criticize the organization, its founding principles, and its culture. Religions are especially sensitive to such criticism.

#5—The Church has increased its transparency

Despite the above points, The Church of Jesus Christ of Latter-day Saints has tried to respond to calls for greater transparency. In 1999, the Church installed a monument at the site of the Meadow Mountain Massacre, recognizing the role of Church members in the tragedy. The Church commissioned its history department to write a four-volume series about Church history called *Saints*. Church historians were told to make the history readable and honest. As of this writing, the Church has made the first three volumes easily accessible. The first book, *Saints, The Standard of Truth* was released in 2018. The latest addition to the series costs about seven dollars, barely covering printing costs. If you want to read the e-books or listen to the audiobooks of *Saints*, they will cost you . . . nothing. The Church is not trying to make money from this series of history books. Authorities of the Church want people to read its history to clear up misperceptions they might still have. The Church also radically changed its website to elucidate its views on current social topics. The Church is not hiding anything. In fact, it is making every effort to be more transparent and participative, a transformation that should be recognized.

PART 2

In Defense of Church Doctrine

Chapter 8

The Nature of God

BEFORE LAUNCHING INTO A DEFENSE OF THE CHURCH OF JESUS CHRIST OF Latter-day Saints, we need to recognize that its doctrine is significantly different from other Christian or Protestant religions. These differences start with our mental image of God and develop from there. As mentioned previously, for the first nineteen years of my life, I attended numerous Protestant churches, including Sunday services, youth classes, and Bible camps. I was taught the following, ancient description of God, still found in *The Westminster Confession of Faith,* chapter 2, written in 1647. Though it has gone through a number of rewritings, the statement is still fairly consistent, and I still remember the teaching. We read,

> There is but one only living and true God, who is infinite in being and perfection, a most pure spirit, invisible, *without body, parts, or passions,* immutable, immense, eternal, incomprehensible, almighty, most wise, most holy, most free, most absolute. (italics added)[29]

By comparison, the doctrine of The Church of Jesus Christ of Latter-day Saints regarding the nature of God may be read in Doctrine and Covenants 130:22.

> The Father has a body of flesh and bones as tangible as man's; the Son also; but the Holy Ghost has not a body of flesh and bones, but is a personage of Spirit. Were it not so, the Holy Ghost could not dwell in us.

Another description of the Savior is given in Doctrine and Covenants 110, when He appeared to Joseph Smith and Oliver Cowdery in the Kirtland temple.

> We saw the Lord standing upon the breastwork of the pulpit, before us; and under his feet was a paved work of pure gold, in color like amber.
>
> His eyes were as a flame of fire; the hair of his head was white like the pure snow; his countenance shone above the brightness of the sun; and his voice was as the sound of the rushing of great waters, even the voice of Jehovah, saying:
>
> I am the first and the last; I am he who liveth, I am he who was slain; I am your advocate with the Father. (D&C 110:2–4)

There is an inescapably huge difference between these two descriptions of our Heavenly Father and the Savior. As such, the Latter-day Saint perception of God is often attacked by other Christian religions. In the opening statement on the topic on one Catholic website we read,

> Certain groups, notably the Mormons, have committed the error of saying that God the Father has a body . . .[30]

From the Latter-day Saint descriptions of God, I now have a mental image of God as a father, or possibly a grandfather, with kind eyes and a brighter countenance than most. He is a person with whom I can talk. Prayers to such a Being are relatively easy, because our relationship will be familiar, yet respectful, much like I have with those people I respect in this life.

Critics often attack this image of a God who has the form of a man with body, parts, and passions. But it was not only Joseph who described God's image as that of a man. We find many examples in the scriptures as well. Only a few such verses from the Bible are provided below to illustrate that God has been considered to have a human form for millennia.

> And God said, Let us make man in our image, after our likeness. (Genesis 1:26)

> And they [Adam and Eve] heard the voice of the Lord God walking in the garden in the cool of the day. (Genesis 3:8)

> And the Lord smelled a sweet savour; and the Lord said in his heart, I will not again curse the ground any more for man's sake; (Genesis 8:21)

> And the Lord spake unto Moses face to face, as a man speaketh unto his friend. (Exodus 33:11)

> For all those things hath mine hand made . . . (Isaiah 66:2)

> When I consider thy heavens, the work of thy fingers, the moon and the stars . . . (Psalms 8:3)

> O sing unto the Lord a new song; for he hath done marvellous things: his right hand, and his holy arm, hath gotten him the victory. (Psalms 98:1)

> And he shall set the sheep on his right hand, but the goats on the left. Then shall the King say unto them on his right hand, Come, ye blessed of my Father, inherit the kingdom prepared for you from the foundation of the world: (Matthew 25:33–34)

None of these verses imply that their references to God's image or body parts are metaphorical. There are simply too many of them to reach such a conclusion.

John 4:24—God is a Spirit

Those who argue that God is spirit and has no body generally base their beliefs on John 4:24, where Jesus says, "God is a Spirit: and they that worship him must worship him in spirit and in truth."

Let's step back a moment and review how this verse came about. If you remember, Jesus was talking with a Samaritan woman at Jacob's well. They had been talking about living water and the fact that this woman had lived with five husbands. Declaring Him to be a prophet, the woman then stated in verse 20,

> Our fathers worshipped in this mountain; and ye say, that in Jerusalem is the place where men ought to worship. (John 4:20)

The mountain to which she referred was Mount Gerizim, considered a holy mountain by the Samaritans and their place to worship. Jews worshipped at the temple in Jerusalem. The Samaritan woman was correct, of course, but Jesus wanted to explain that things were changing. In verse 23, He states,

> But the hour cometh, and now is, when the true worshippers shall worship the Father in spirit and in truth: for the Father seeketh such to worship him. (John 4:23)

With the coming of the Savior's gospel, one did not have to go to a particular place to worship. The Samaritans would not have to climb Mount

Gerizim and Jews would not have to travel to Jerusalem. They could worship through the spirit, not through burnt sacrifices. This was a profound change in the prescribed method of worship for both religions. Jesus's next four words were either a giant departure from their discussion topic—or a continuation of how true worship was to now take place. The Savior says,

> God is a Spirit: and they that worship him must worship him in spirit and in truth. (John 4:24)

Jesus had just been explaining a major change in the way the Samaritans and everyone else would now worship. Nowhere in the Old Testament had it been taught that God was a spirit. Was Jesus announcing a major change in our understanding of the nature of God? Or was He continuing the lesson that God was now to be worshipped spiritually? The Savior immediately continues with His teaching about this new way of worshipping God, apparently without even starting a new sentence. He continues, "and they that worship him must worship him in spirit and in truth."

The Joseph Smith translation of John 4:24 adds a similar clarification to the Savior's statement.

> For unto such hath God promised his Spirit. And they who worship him, must worship in spirit and in truth.

The extra few words added by Joseph strengthens the conclusion that Jesus stayed on topic and did not divert the discussion to a major new revelation of only four words.

The mental image of God having the physical appearance of being a man is important, because it provides a foundation for the rest of the gospel. With that image in mind, it is easier to relate to God, understand the need for church and temple attendance, value family support, and reject degrading and reprehensible behavior. We worship an exalted man who is now a god, not an invisible spirit that is spread out through the universe.

Many critics of Latter-day Saint doctrine proclaim that the Church is trying to bring God down to man's level. That idea is incorrect. We are not trying to bring God down to our level. We are trying to elevate ourselves—eventually—up to His. We will discuss more on this topic in the chapter on becoming as Gods.

Many people seem surprised that The Church of Jesus Christ of Latter-day Saints is not adjusting its doctrine to better mainstream itself with other Christian religions. However, God has already let His wishes be known about this idea. When Jesus Christ appeared to Joseph Smith, Joseph asked Him which of all the sects was right and which he should join. Jesus answered that Joseph must join none of them, for they were all wrong and, in fact, their creeds were an abomination in His sight.[31] Should it surprise us then that Latter-day Saint doctrine differs from all other religions? In doing their missionary work, Church members often try to minimize those differences. But sometimes in our discussions we must recognize our doctrinal differences with other religions—and then be willing to explain and defend them.

Chapter 9

The Gospel Topics Essays

The Pew Research Center is an organization that conducts telephone surveys to determine the opinions and practices of populations across the world. The Center asks people about their religious beliefs and observance. Across all Christian religions, the Center has found that church members are abandoning their beliefs and listing themselves as unaffiliated with any religion.

This disaffiliation is significantly correlated with the age of the respondent. As you will see in the table below, the religiously unaffiliated of the oldest, Silent Generation (born between 1928 and 1945) has barely changed from 2007 to 2019. On the other hand, the unaffiliated from the Millennial generation has increased from 25% to 40% over the same time period.[32]

Generational Differences of Religiously Unaffiliated			
Pew Research Center Survey Results			
	2007	2014	2019
Silent Generation	9%	11%	10%
Baby Boomers	14%	17%	17%
Generation X	19%	23%	25%
Millennials	25%	34%	40%

The Church of Jesus Christ of Latter-day Saints has not been immune to this same trend. In her excellent book, *The Next Mormons,* Jana Riess conducted her own survey of Latter-day Saints in 2016. Among other questions, she asked if the respondent was confident that Jesus Christ was resurrected, that there is life after death, that Joseph Smith was a prophet, and that the Book of Mormon is a true account. The results were as follows.[33]

Generational Differences of Confidence in Latter-day Saint Religious Beliefs				
from The Next Mormons				
	Resurrected Jesus Christ	Life After Death	Joseph Smith	Book of Mormon
Silent / Boomers	83%	80%	67%	62%
Generation X	70%	70%	54%	53%
Millennials	57%	62%	51%	50%

With this drop in confidence in Latter-day Saint tenets came a corresponding drop in church attendance, prayer, and obedience to practices specific to the Latter-day Saint faith, such as the Word of Wisdom. The Church recognized this disaffiliation. Obviously, Millennials were leaving all Christian churches, however, Church leaders could not simply chalk up the abandonment to societal changes and not respond to it. The Church had been under verbal and written attacks from books, podcasts, blogs, websites, and social media for many decades. Historically, the Church had not responded to such criticisms. However, the attacks were appearing on every social media outlet and our young adults were being influenced.

In October 2012, Elder Quentin L. Cook gave a conference talk that openly recognized the problem the Church was facing. Speaking mostly of younger adult members, he stated,

> Some have immersed themselves in Internet materials that magnify, exaggerate, and, in some cases, invent shortcomings of early Church leaders. Then they draw incorrect conclusions that can affect testimony.[34]

As mentioned previously, the Church initiated programs to be more openly transparent about its beliefs and history. In a landmark address at the general conference in October 2013, Elder Dieter Uchtdorf added his contribution to the new policy.

> We openly acknowledge that in nearly 200 years of Church history—along with an uninterrupted line of inspired, honorable, and divine events—there have been some things said and done that could cause people to question. . . .
>
> And, to be perfectly frank, there have been times when members or leaders in the Church have simply made mistakes.

> There may have been things said or done that were not in harmony with our values, principles, or doctrine.[35]

A number of changes were made as the Church strived to become more open about Church history and doctrine. The policy of avoiding discussions about difficult moments in its history was changed. As mentioned earlier, the Church commissioned its history department to write a new four-volume series about Church history called *Saints*. The Church also published a series of written documents about specific Church doctrines called the "Gospel Topics Essays." The first Gospel Topic Essay was posted on the Church website in November 2013. The twelfth and final essay was posted in October 2015. Taken from the introduction to the Gospel Topics Essays on the Church website, we read,

> Recognizing that today so much information about The Church of Jesus Christ of Latter- day Saints can be obtained from questionable and often inaccurate sources, officials of the Church began in 2013 to publish straightforward, in-depth essays on a number of topics. The purpose of these essays . . . has been to gather accurate information from many different sources and publications and place it in the Gospel Topics section of ChurchofJesusChrist.org . . .[36]

The Church chose topics for these essays based on the most serious and widespread complaints of disenchanted members. The essays give us some insight as to what aspects of Church doctrine and history were most bothersome to members of the Millennial generation. The essays also demonstrate that Church leadership had become aware of the crisis it faced and was taking steps to address it.

The Essays were written, of course, to provide honest answers to questions and attacks by critics which are still widely distributed on social media. The answers were carefully and patiently worded. However, for the purposes of this book, I would like to look at the questions themselves. Are the questions fair? What are the assumptions behind each of them? Our serpent side may wish to question the questions before trying to answer them.

The following is a listing of the titles of the Gospel Topics Essays. In the next several chapters, we will consider these questions in a slightly different light, using the Gospel Topics Essays as references for this assessment.

- Essay 1—Are Mormons Christian?
- Essay 2—Becoming Like God
- Essay 3—Book of Mormon and DNA Studies

- Essay 4—Book of Mormon Translation
- Essay 5—First Vision Accounts
- Essay 6—Joseph Smith's Teachings about Priesthood, Temple, and Women
- Essay 7—Mother in Heaven
- Essay 8—Peace and Violence among 19th-Century Latter-day Saints
- Essay 9—Plural Marriage in The Church of Jesus Christ of Latter-day Saints Plural Marriage Kirtland and Nauvoo
    - Plural Marriage and Families in Early Utah
    - The Manifesto and the End of Plural Marriage
- Essay 10—Race and the Priesthood
- Essay 11—Translation and Historicity of the Book of Abraham[37]

Chapter 10

You Are Not Allowed to Redefine My Words

The first topic in the Gospel Topics Essays addresses the question, "Are Mormons Christian?" When I first heard this query voiced, my initial response was, "Well of course Mormons are Christian. What a ridiculous question." As mentioned previously, in religious discussions, questions are often debate ploys. If one hears a question often enough, you will begin to wonder why it is still being asked, making you wonder if the obvious answer is incorrect. If attackers of the Latter-day Saint faith can continue to ask the question, "Are Mormons Christian?", it makes Church missionary work more difficult and damages public opinion.

Obviously, Church members have fully answered the question many times by simply referring to a dictionary. The definition of Christian is "a person who believes in Jesus Christ; adherent of Christianity."[38] Another is "A Christian is defined as a person who believes in the teachings of Jesus Christ and who has accepted Christ as his/her savior."[39] But critics of Latter-day Saint doctrine, perhaps not realizing that they have no authority to change the definition of words, doggedly answer this question with a "No," despite all evidence. By redefining the word "Christian" to exclude Latter-day Saint doctrine, they believe they can prove The Church of Jesus Christ of Latter-day Saints is not Christian. As Church members, we must refuse to accept this definition.

To illustrate this tactic, did your children ever try to play the No-Means-Yes game with you? One day, my young daughter and her little brother casually entered the family room and sat on the couch across from me. My daughter took the role of spokesperson. The conversation went something like this . . .

"Daddy, let's pretend we live in a world where Yes means No and No means Yes."

"Okay . . ." I responded, seeing all kinds of danger in this line of thinking. But, hey, you want to be a good sport and encourage your children's imagination, right? My young son asked a couple of nonsense questions, like "Does two plus two equal four?", to which I answered "No." Lots of silly laughter ensued.

"So, Daddy, can we have ice cream?" my daughter asked innocently.

"Yes . . . ?" I responded cautiously, still following the rules of the new game.

With a delighted squeal, my two children jumped off the couch and ran into the kitchen. "Mommy, Daddy said we could have ice cream!" they announced, gleeful in their wit and clever ploy to get me to verbally agree to a mid-afternoon treat. Even today, my children still believe they are hilarious.

However, the Yes-Means-No game illustrates the importance of maintaining the definitions of the words we use. Once you agree to a new definition of terms, it's very hard to back out of that commitment.

This is the case when answering the question, "Are Mormons Christian?" Such an interrogation may go as follows.

"Are Mormons Christian?" your questioner asks.

"Yes, we are," you respond confidently. "The name of our church is The Church of Jesus Christ of Latter-day Saints. We believe that Jesus Christ is the Savior of the world, whose coming was foretold throughout the Old Testament. His birth, adult life, miracles, and teachings are recorded in the New Testament. We seek to follow His teachings, church organization, and ordinances."

If your questioner genuinely wants to know if Mormons are Christian, he will thank you for your answer and that will be the end of it. After all, everyone knows the meaning of the word "Christian," and your answer demonstrates that Jesus Christ is the center of the Latter-day Saint religion. So, why is this question still being asked, when the answer is so obvious? Because the Latter-day Saint faith is a much better target if its Christianity is called into question. Critics of the Church want to remove the Latter-day Saint religion from the list of Christian religions that exist in the world today.

To have any chance at supporting their claim that Mormons are not Christian, critics must resort to redefining the word "Christian." For example, your questioner may ask, "Do you believe in the Jesus Christ whose life and teachings may *only* be found in the New Testament and not in your Book of Mormon?" or "Do you believe that God the Father and Jesus

Christ are one incorporeal being without body, parts, or passions who exists throughout the breadth of the universe?"

If you exclaim, "No, we don't believe in such descriptions of Jesus Christ!", your interrogator may immediately conclude, "Then Mormons are not Christian."

Your interviewer has imposed his own religious beliefs into a faulty definition of Jesus Christ and what it means to be a Christian. Like the No-Means-Yes game, you must verbally declare that you will not accept a new definition of the word "Christian." You are on very solid ground in your response, as no dictionary or encyclopedia has ever used your interrogator's definition either. By definition, Mormons are certainly Christians. We must recognize and call out our interviewers if they try to redefine the meanings of words.

Words are Important

For a week during my time in graduate school, I got sick with the flu. It was the bad, multi- symptom type of flu—nausea, headache, watering eyes, and wracking cough. I couldn't read, but I was so bored I finally resorted to watching daytime television. I came upon an episode of a talk show hosted by Phil Donahue. In his show, Donahue allowed audience members to participate in the discussion. When I tuned in, the show had just started, but the audience was already very agitated. Donahue's guests were a man and two women who all lived together—and claimed that they were "married." It turns out they dated other people occasionally as well.

The audience was all kinds of upset. I laid there in bed thinking my illness was preventing me from grasping the point of their anger. Audience members would admit they did not care what this threesome did behind closed doors. This was not moral outrage at three people who were disobeying the law of chastity. I finally realized the audience was upset because this threesome insisted on calling their relationship a marriage. The audience's definition of marriage did not include a threesome that dated around when they felt like it. Most of the audience was married and they understood the sacrifice and loyalty that marriage requires. The word "marriage" and the loyalty required by it were important to them, and these three guests were trampling on a concept that they held sacred. In my semi-lucid state of health, I remember wanting to make a phone call to the show and explain my epiphany so everyone could calm down and stop arguing.

Words are important. They carry meaning. In business meetings, when I hear the suggestion to "not get caught up in the semantics," I cringe. If we didn't all agree on the terms we were using, how can we know we are communicating?

In any religious discussion, keep in mind that words and even mental images are important. There are many people who only think of the Savior at Christmas time. Consequently, their image of the Savior is that of a newborn baby. What could be less intimidating than a baby? If they believe in a Final Judgment, those who associate Jesus Christ with a newborn aren't going to be particularly worried. Similarly, if you only associate Jesus Christ as always being dovelike, you won't be too concerned either.

If you are talking to someone who thinks of Jesus Christ as a pushover, getting her to think of Him as the Being who will hold her accountable in the Final Judgment may be difficult. There is still plenty of disagreement surrounding the definitions of the words Christian, Jesus Christ, saints, gospel, Sabbath, restoration, and many others. In conclusion, hold fast to your definitions of the words used in discussing gospel doctrine. Beware of those who would redefine those words in order to advance their own arguments.

Chapter 11

Prophets and Revelation

On October 15, 1985, two separate pipe bombs exploded in the Salt Lake City area, killing Steve Christensen and Kathy Sheets, the wife of Gary Sheets. The next day, another pipe bomb exploded in the car of Mark Hofmann, badly injuring him. Thus began an intense investigation into the man Mark Hofmann, an antiquities dealer who specialized in finding and selling historical documents of his church, The Church of Jesus Christ of Latter-day Saints.

Mark Hofmann first met with the First Presidency of the Church on April 22, 1980. Specifically, he met with Spencer W. Kimball, N. Eldon Tanner, Marion G. Romney, Gordon B. Hinckley, Boyd K. Packer, and a number of men who worked for the Church Historical Department. They met to examine a document that came to be known as the Anthon transcript. Purportedly this was the document that Martin Harris took to Professor Charles Anthon in New York for his expert verification of hieroglyphic characters from the Book of Mormon and Joseph Smith's translation.[40] Actually, the paper was a forgery of that document made by Mark Hofmann.[41]

For the next five years, Mark Hofmann would have meetings with other Church officials, including Gordon B. Hinckley, Dallin H. Oaks, and Hugh Pinnock. Besides the Anthon transcript, he sold several other forgeries to the Church, including the infamous "White Salamander Letter." For several years, the Salamander Letter provoked concern and debate throughout the Church, though it turned out to be a forgery. Finally, Hofmann tried to sell, sight unseen, a collection of journals and letters purportedly written by William E. McLellin. As mentioned previously, McLellin was an early convert to the Church who had been an apostle for three years, but eventually joined the Missouri mobs against the Church and was excommunicated.[42]

But this particular swindle went horribly wrong for Hofmann. He tried to cover his tracks with pipe bombs. The rest is history.

The news media swarmed all over the story of course. Three pipe bomb explosions, two murders, and a history of antiquities forgeries provided an exciting story. But journalists went further than just reporting the news. They thought their readers would enjoy hearing that the leadership of the Church may have played a part in the felonies. As described by Church historian Richard E. Turley,

> Similarly, church officials' roles were misconstrued. Many news reports were couched in ambiguous terms that stopped short of accusing them of ordering the bombings yet allowed for the possibility. One story began, "Bombings, killings, connected to the Mormon Church? What in the world is going on in Utah?"[43]

Sadly enough, we seem to live in a world where people want to discover that religious leaders are tainted and sinful. None of the insinuations of these news reports were true of course.

Church leaders had acted in the best interest of our faith, trying to collect documents important in Church history. Today, however, Church critics still point to the Mark Hofmann story as proof that The Church of Jesus Christ of Latter-day Saints is not an inspired institution.

If Spencer W. Kimball and Gordon B. Hinckley were actually prophets, then why didn't God reveal the truth about Mark Hofmann to them? The assumption here is that God continually provides streams of revelation and, if the prophet doesn't know the future, he is simply not paying attention. This assumption has been made numerous times in Church history. However, this is a flawed perception that has no foundation in the scriptures. Otherwise, the prophets of old would have been much better informed.

For example, in Exodus chapter 18, Moses's father-in-law, Jethro, watched as Moses sat in judgment over the people all day long.

> And Moses' father-in-law said unto him, The thing that thou doest is not good.
>
> Thou wilt surely wear away, both thou, and this people that is with thee: for this thing is too heavy for thee; thou art not able to perform it thyself alone. . . .
>
> Moreover thou shalt provide out of all the people able men, such as fear God, men of truth, hating covetousness; and place such over them, to be rulers of thousands, and rulers of hundreds, rulers of fifties, and rulers of tens:

> And let them judge the people at all seasons: and it shall be, that every great matter they shall bring unto thee, but every small matter they shall judge: so shall it be easier for thyself, and they shall bear the burden with thee. (Exodus 18:17–18, 21–22)

Moses was overextending himself trying to sit as judge over thousands of people. But the Lord did not give him the counsel to organize other leaders and judges. Jethro had to approach his son-in-law to help Moses avoid an emotional breakdown.

In Matthew 26:39, the Savior is praying in the Garden of Gethsemane. We read,

> And he went a little further, and fell on his face, and prayed, saying, O my Father, if it be possible, let this cup pass from me: nevertheless not as I will, but as thou wilt.

For many years, this verse confused me. Why would the Savior even ask such a thing? The Atonement was the key to God's children attaining immortal life. Finally, I realized the Savior asked the question for the same reason anyone asks a question—because *He didn't know the answer.* It had not been revealed to Him. Living by faith requires that you don't know the whole story. That requirement apparently exists whether you are a lay member, a prophet, or the Son of God.

In Acts chapter 10, Peter receives a full-fledged vision telling him to take the gospel to the Gentiles. Yet the policy of whether Gentiles were required to be circumcised upon baptism was still an open question. This became a major controversy between the Jewish and the Gentile converts in the church. Finally, a church conference was called to decide the matter. In Acts 15, we read the words of Peter, as he expressed his opinion on the matter,

> Now therefore why tempt ye God, to put a yoke upon the neck of the disciples, which neither our fathers nor we were able to bear? (Acts 15:10)

Peter gives the church his own argument here, but never claims that it came by revelation. He actually asks his brethren, in essence, "Shouldn't we consider the matter this way?" It seems apparent that God didn't provide Peter with revelation even though circumcision was a major issue for the early church.

In Acts chapter seven, we read about Steven, an assistant to the twelve apostles and a missionary for the early church of Jesus Christ. He saw a vision of God the Father and Jesus Christ and publicly announced his vision, for which he was stoned to death. Why didn't God warn Steven to not declare his vision, which led to his immediate death?

In the first chapter of Helaman we read about Pahoran the second, who had just been elected to be the chief judge to replace his father. Couldn't the Lord have warned Pahoran that he was about to be assassinated by Kishkumen? The Lord had previously warned the Nephite prophets about movements by the Lamanite army. Yet He didn't warn Helaman that a Lamanite army was marching upon Zarahemla and would soon defeat and occupy it.

God didn't reveal the plans of the Japanese military to attack Pearl Harbor on December 7, 1942. He didn't reveal the plans of nineteen terrorists to hijack four airliners and crash them into the New York Trade Center and the Pentagon on September 11, 2001. The requirements of Earth life forbid such interference by the Lord. Only rarely will He reveal oncoming disasters.

It's easy to jump to speculation about what God is thinking. We may feel like we know our Heavenly Father well enough to speak for Him. However, it's just not a good idea. God has told us that we shouldn't speculate on what He is thinking. He has more knowledge and perspective than we do. He understands the rules of earth life. In Isaiah, we read,

> For my thoughts are not your thoughts, neither are your ways my ways, saith the Lord.
>
> For as the heavens are higher than the earth, so are my ways higher than your ways, and my thoughts than your thoughts. (Isaiah 55:8–9)

The Lord does *not* provide the prophet with nearly as much revelation as many seem to think He does. The Lord usually lets each of us work out our individual problems so that we can grow and learn. Likewise, the Lord lets his prophet and church leadership grapple with problems so they and the membership can grow and learn.

The belief that a prophet should know everything the Lord knows has existed since the early days of the restored church. Symonds Ryder was baptized into the Church while living in Hiram, Ohio. Though he was apparently having other doubts about the Church, Ryder reportedly decided to apostatize when his mission call arrived with his name misspelled. Church members still take offense at such menial offenses today, based on their belief that Church leaders should be inspired in all things. However, history teaches us that God does not take the responsibility to warn mankind, or even His church, about oncoming disasters.

So, how did the Mark Hofmann saga end? Did the Church learn anything? In a talk given at Brigham Young University in August 1987 and later reprinted in the *Ensign* magazine, Dallin H. Oaks summarized his conclusions regarding Mark Hoffman.

> In his crimes against person and property, he had many victims, the Church being only one among many. When it comes to naivete in the face of malevolence, there is blame enough to go around. We all need to be more cautious.[44]

In his excellent book *Victims—The LDS Church and the Mark Hofmann Case,* Richard E. Turley agrees with Elder Oaks that the Church had indeed learned a painful but needed lesson from this experience,

> Both by examining documents themselves and submitting them to outside experts for analysis, church officials also began taking advantage of the new forgery detection techniques developed by forensic examiners in the case. The Historical Department refined its acquisition procedures, carefully documenting all manuscripts received and giving greater emphasis than ever to provenance. Most of all, perhaps, church officials developed increased skepticism toward accepting new and startling document discoveries.[45]

So, yes, even a worldwide church can learn important lessons from horrendous and costly experiences. The Lord is not going to spare His church from such growth opportunities. In summary, one must look at the assumptions behind questions and attacks upon the Church. God chooses what revelations to communicate to Church leaders. To think that Latter-day Saint leaders are not doing their jobs since they don't know everything is not supported by doctrine, the scriptures, historical evidence, or common sense.

Chapter 12

Responding to Emotion-Based Criticism

MANY CRITICISMS OF THE CHURCH ARE DIFFICULT TO DEBATE, BECAUSE there are few scriptures or revelations that address them. One might call these issues emotion-based criticisms because there are no facts on which to base a logical debate. Emotion-based criticisms against the Church are becoming more common, because as stated earlier, critics are becoming more emotional.

To calmly recognize and respond to such attacks, Church members should not let themselves be caught up in an emotional exchange. An emotional response to an emotional critique does no one any good. As discussed in previous chapters, emotional attacks are often about how a Church leader or member has mistreated someone. For that particular criticism, the best answer is that, no, Latter-day Saints are not perfect and many of us would be rated below average in social skills and empathy. It's the truth, it's logical, and it should put the argument to rest.

However, some emotional attacks are more complex and directed at Church doctrine. Let's discuss how one might handle such questions.

BECOMING LIKE GOD

You will find that emotion-based criticisms are often used in discussions about deeper Latter-day Saint doctrines. Deeper doctrines include eternal life, eternal families, Heavenly Mother, and temple covenants. These concepts are above and beyond what the Savior could teach to His mostly uneducated followers in Palestine. These deeper doctrines tend to be unique to The Church of Jesus Christ of Latter-day Saints and are subject to robust criticism. However, since there are no scriptures that argue against the doctrines, it is hard for critics to mount a scripturally based attack on them.

Latter-day Saint doctrine that eternal progression allows us to become gods draws a number of emotional attacks. This belief is a favorite target for critics of the Church, mainly due to the perceived impertinence of the doctrine. You can recognize emotion-based arguments because they state no facts and make no actual points that might be rebutted. Emotional arguments sound something like this:

> "The Mormons think that they can become like God, or gods themselves! This doctrine is arrogant as well as ridiculous!"
>
> "LDS members try to deny this doctrine, but don't you believe them. There are plenty of quotes by LDS leaders that the Mormon church believes that they will become like gods!"
>
> "It's just mind-blowing that the Mormons think that they can become gods! Who would believe in such nonsense?"

The emotional argument is essentially built upon the same reasoning that cheerleaders use at a college football game. Cheerleaders want you to clap your hands till they hurt and scream until you are hoarse. They want you to stay on your feet the whole game (though you probably paid a lot of money to rent that seat). Cheerleaders don't *logically* argue that you should damage your hands, voice, and feet. They must instead appeal to your *emotions* of team loyalty. Likewise, the emotional argument seeks the listener's emotional response. Critics of Latter-day Saint doctrine want their listeners to be outraged, offended, and astonished by Latter-day Saint doctrine. They want their audience slapping their foreheads in disbelief.

As stated, because the doctrine that we can become as God is a more advanced, meat-of-the- gospel principle, there are few Biblical scriptures about the doctrine. Since there are no scriptures about the teaching, there are also very few alternative doctrines regarding the belief. Thus, critics of Latter-day Saint doctrine must resort to the emotional argument, because raising a logical argument is simply not possible.

To counter the emotional argument, one must direct the discussion back into a more reasonable path. There are two ways to do this. For many such rants, you may simply ask the question, "Do you have a reference for any of your points?" Since your questioner is resorting to an emotional argument, there are almost certainly no scriptures to back the criticism. They may try to quote other critics like themselves, but referencing the statements of fellow critics does not build their case.

Secondly, if your interrogator is simply attacking our church doctrine regarding the afterlife, you may ask him what his belief is in regard to the disputed doctrine. In my discussions with Christians who are incredulous about the fact that Latter-day Saints believe they can become as gods, I have asked, "So what do *you* believe happens in the afterlife? Once you have been resurrected, judged, and have received your eternal reward . . . what *will* you do for all eternity?" I have never received an answer to this question. Our post-earth life is a huge mystery to the Christian world, because there are so few scriptures about the afterlife. Most Christians imagine we will be dressed in white robes, lounging on clouds, singing in choirs, and maybe discussing doctrine. A couple of my less aggressive non-Latter-day Saint friends have admitted, "I have wondered about that question many times in my life."

Logically, the concept of eternal progress rather demands that we can become gods. What else can justify an eternity of effort? If there is no eternal progress towards becoming like our Heavenly Father, how will we not get bored and fall into despair? How could we *not* want to leave such a repetitious, unmeaningful existence? As my wife puts it, we can't dust the clouds and sing in heavenly choirs for eternity. She has a good point. I don't like housework and I don't have a good singing voice. I would become bitter at the thought that I lived a life of sacrifice and righteousness on earth in order to attain a very boring afterlife. Not only is the doctrine of eternal life logical, it's also the most awe-inspiring of all our beliefs. It promises me an eternity of learning and accomplishing meaningful work.

The response to an emotional argument such as this is simple, but a little scary. In many such cases, you should simply agree with your opponent. Yes, The Church of Jesus Christ of Latter- day Saints believes that we can become gods. President Lorenzo Snow really *did* make the statement, "As man now is, God once was: As God now is, man may be."[46] This statement is an essential part of the doctrine of our belief in eternal progression. We must progress towards *something* and becoming like God is the only goal worthy of an eternity of effort. Members of The Church of Jesus Christ of Latter-day Saints should not deny, or apologize for, their doctrine.

Heavenly Mother

This same approach may be used if someone attacks our doctrine of a Heavenly Mother. First, we should admit up front that we believe in the concept of a heavenly mother, but we have very little information about Her. A heavenly mother is first mentioned in a Church hymn entitled "O My Father." Its lyrics were written by Eliza R. Snow, who felt inspired to write her poem after Joseph Smith had taught her the principle of heavenly parents. There are no scriptures that deny the presence of a heavenly mother, so any criticism of the doctrine must fall into the category of emotional argument. Again, it is a rather logical doctrine. If we have a Heavenly Father, couldn't one expect that we have a Heavenly Mother as well?

I have heard the argument that we know so little about Heavenly Mother because Heavenly Father does not want Her name to be dragged through the mud like His and Jesus Christ's. If you think for a moment of all the profanities that include the name Jesus or God, you'll see the point of this argument. Mankind has a hard time giving proper respect to the most sacred things of life. Was I God, I too would try to keep the existence of a Heavenly Mother secret.

The Latter-day Saint belief about a heavenly mother is well known, and one should never deny the doctrine. One of the Gospel Topics Essays reviews the history of this doctrine and explains what we know.[47] With so very little data or scriptural references, this belief must remain in the category of emotional argument. As such, if someone attacks our doctrine of a Heavenly Mother, it is better to simply agree to disagree. Yes, the Church does have that doctrine and it is a rather logical extension of our belief in eternal families. Personally, the doctrines that we can become as gods, that we have a Heavenly Mother, and that we can make covenants with Heavenly Father that are binding after death take my breath away. What a wonderful and fascinating gospel.

Chapter 13

Responding to Science-Based Criticism

Of all the arguments used against the Church, the scientific argument is one of the more difficult to counter. Unless you have a passing understanding of the controversy and the science behind it, you can find yourself at a loss of what to say. Attacks on religion due to new findings in science are not rare, but they are not as common as they once were. For decades the Church had to answer questions about evolution. A couple of our Church leaders made conservative comments against evolution, which made the Church a target for criticism that still linger today. However, the debate between evolution and creationism was founded on the question of whether God exists. It was not founded on specific Latter-day Saint doctrine.

Your ability to find the faulty assumptions and faulty logic behind a science-based criticism depends on how familiar you are with the topic. You should never be intimidated by the science behind a religious debate—because you don't need to remember the details of the science. For most such science-based criticisms, you only need to remember a basic, single-sentence summary of the faulty assumptions behind the complaint. If you understand the fatal flaw behind a science-based attack on the existence of God or of a true religion, you can give a satisfactory answer to the question. To illustrate that fact, I would like to present two examples of science-based questioning of the Church and the summary statements that answer them. The first attack started in 1859 and called into question the existence of God. The other accusation is quite a bit more recent and attacked the validity of the Book of Mormon.

Evolution vs. Creationism

In the Evolution vs. Genesis debate, our main character is Charles Darwin, who was born in England in 1809. He graduated from Cambridge in 1831, ironically with plans to become a clergyman. But that same year, Darwin's interest in geology and natural history won him an appointment as the naturalist on the surveying ship H.M.S. Beagle, bound for South America. What first appeared to be a simple diversion in Darwin's life led to a fire storm of events. From observations developed on his voyage to the Galapagos Islands and South America, Darwin published the theory of evolution in 1859. His now-famous book, *On the Origin of Species by Means of Natural Selection,* was a smashing success. His first edition sold out immediately and evolution made headlines. As Darwin had feared, members of the social elite, scientists, and celebrities worldwide hailed the book as the discovery of a lifetime and that it removed the need for God in the creation of our world.

Demonstrations for and against evolution continued for decades. School boards hostilely debated if evolution should be taught in schools. In 1925, the state of Tennessee prosecuted a teacher named John Scopes for teaching evolution in high school. The trial, commonly referred to as the Scopes Monkey Trial, captured national attention and was seen as a contest between the faithful followers of God and disbelieving evolutionists. They even made a movie about it.[48]

But, amid the uproar, data kept coming in. Tons of fossils were discovered. Carbon dating of the organic material and uranium-lead dating of the inorganics in fossils was published. The results continued to point to an earth that was billions of years old. Then DNA sequencing confirmed the proposed routes of evolution and their approximate time frames so convincingly that all those collected fossils are no longer necessary to prove the case for evolution. Gradually, the general public accepted the realities of these scientific advances. Today, the basic tenets of evolution, as proposed by Charles Darwin, are no longer being debated in scientific circles. The 4.5-billion-year age of the earth is no longer questioned either. There is simply too much data supporting both conclusions. The book of Genesis breaks up the Creation into six periods, but there are few people today who still believe those intervals were six 24-hour days.

Evolution is a wonderful, complex tool needed to put life of every kind onto a lifeless planet. I fully support the science of evolution. But the belief that random chance directed evolution instead of God is . . . quite impossible. Being a very complex tool, evolution requires a Being with a high level of intelligence to wield it. Random chance is not nearly smart enough.

This is the fatal flaw of critics who wish to use evolution to prove that God does not exist. The idea that something as complex as the human brain could evolve from non-living raw materials through a series of billions of lucky, random chances is . . . very, very unlikely.

So, if someone ever questions you about how evolution and religion fit together, you must only remember one argument. First, I suggest you agree with your challenger that evolution is a critical tool required by the Creation. The argument that you must remember in such discussions is that evolution *needed to be directed.* Atheistic evolutionists must promote random chance as the Director of Evolution because they have no other choice. It is, however, a poor and terribly illogical choice.

Perhaps a brief overview of the technical complexity of the Creation is in order. Before the Big Bang, matter did not exist. Equally importantly, the laws of physics that dictate the form and interactions of matter didn't exist. The Big Bang was a colossal release of untold amounts of energy to create everything in the universe. After that event, matter existed, with very precise dimensions, charges, and energies. For example, a single proton has a mass of 1.67262 × 10–27 kg. What if protons had a slightly higher mass? Such a change would increase the mass-to- charge ratio of protons, which would affect the strong nuclear force and weak nuclear force that holds the nuclei of atoms together. That change would in turn change the electromagnetic forces holding atoms together as well as how atoms bond to become molecules. Yet, if you change how molecules bind even slightly, carbon-based biology is severely affected. Life becomes impossible.

Or let's go big and change the gravitational constant. Suns, which are the home of continuous thermonuclear fusion reactions, are held together by gravity. Increase it and suns burn out too quickly for evolution to occur on their planets. Decrease it and many suns don't form at all.

Similar catastrophes occur by changing any of the hundreds of particle masses, charges, and interactions. Change energies of the electromagnetic spectrum, gravity, or other form of radiation and you will also create a new and unique universe—which will almost certainly *not* support life. How fine-tuned was the Big Bang to produce a universe with exactly the right settings for the development and support of humankind? To create something as tremendously complex as the earth, plant life, bacteria, animals, and mankind, requires a director who is much more knowledgeable than random selection. In fact, such a director needs to have the wisdom and power of God.

DNA and the Book of Mormon

In the year 2000, a charge was made that the rapidly developing technology of DNA sequencing had turned up evidence to discredit the Book of Mormon. To understand this charge, we need to review the utility of DNA sequencing in . . . genealogy.

Genealogists are well aware that DNA sequencing may be used to identify from where in the world your ancestors originated. Those of you who have had your DNA sequenced know that you must simply collect saliva in a small test tube and send it to a genetics lab. For a small fee, the DNA of the body cells suspended in that saliva will be sequenced, providing you with the order of the nucleic acids that make up your DNA. In the course of sequencing the DNA of millions of people, geneticists have found that there are certain unique series of nucleic acids that are associated with a given part of the world. There are DNA sequences specific to, say, Northern Europe, or Africa, or Turkey. So, if your ancestors came from Turkey, you will have some sequences of DNA native to Turkey. A computer analysis of your DNA sequence of nucleic acids uncovers how many such unique sequences you have (say, from Turkey). With a little math, the program calculates what percentage of your DNA comes from Turkey and how much from other locations.

As DNA sequencing progressed over the last fifty years, critics of Latter-day Saint doctrine announced that DNA evidence proved that Lehi and his family could not have immigrated to the New World, as claimed by the Book of Mormon. DNA found in the indigenous peoples of Mesoamerica does not contain DNA sequences that are common to the peoples of the Near East and Jerusalem. If the indigenous people of the Americas really descended from an immigrant people from Jerusalem, critics declared that DNA sequences common to Jerusalem must be found in their DNA.

As an aside, within the DNA of indigenous Americans was found DNA sequences common to peoples of *Southeast Asia*. This was not really a surprise. For decades, archeologists have taught the Bering Land Bridge Theory. During the world's ice ages, water was frozen into ice sheets and glaciers, shrinking the oceans, and exposing a land bridge from Russia to Alaska. The first Americans were believed to be nomadic Asian tribes who either crossed over that land bridge or took a boat. These immigrations occurred over thousands of years. For example, the so-called Kennewick Man is the 9,000-year-old skeleton of a man named for the location in Washington state where he was found. It appears he too had descended from a people who originated on the coasts of Asia. Such findings indicate that for millennia, people have immigrated to the Americas, established civilizations, and moved throughout the two American continents.

For years, many members of the Church believed and taught that *all* indigenous peoples of the Americas were direct descendants of the Lamanite people. If that was true . . . if Father Lehi and Ishmael really were the ancestors of all the indigenous peoples of the Americas, then the DNA of the indigenous people absolutely *should* contain DNA sequences common to the Near East and Jerusalem.

The findings of DNA studies forced the Church to reevaluate the belief that the American Indians were all descendants of the Lamanites. In 2006, the Church made a slight but significant change in the Introduction of the Book of Mormon, which rather signaled their decision. The sentence once read, "After thousands of years, all were destroyed except the Lamanites, and they are the *principal* ancestors of the American Indians." It now reads, "After thousands of years, all were destroyed except the Lamanites, and they *are among* the ancestors of the American Indians" (italics added).

This question became such an issue for the Church that at the end of 2014, the essay entitled "Book of Mormon and DNA Studies" was included in the Gospel Topics Essays. It's an interesting read and is available on the Church website. In that paper, the Church makes the following declarations:

> The Book of Mormon provides little direct information about cultural contact between the peoples it describes and others who may have lived nearby. Consequently, most early Latter-day Saints assumed that Near Easterners or West Asians like Jared, Lehi, Mulek, and their companions were the first or the largest or even the only groups to settle the Americas. . . .
>
> The Book of Mormon itself, however, does not claim that the peoples it describes were either the predominant or the exclusive inhabitants of the lands they occupied. In fact, cultural and demographic clues in its text hint at the presence of other groups. . . .
>
> . . . Nothing is known about the extent of intermarriage and genetic mixing between Book of Mormon peoples or their descendants and other inhabitants of the Americas, though some mixing appears evident, even during the period covered by the book's text. What seems clear is that the DNA of Book of Mormon peoples likely represented only a fraction of all DNA in ancient America.[49]

This DNA evidence confirmed (and, admittedly, accelerated) the belief of many Book of Mormon scholars that the Nephites and Lamanites made up only a small fraction of the total number of inhabitants of the Americas. Let's look at what archeology has revealed.

We know the small area of land in Mesoamerica where the Book of Mormon narration took place was inhabited by other peoples as well. Archeology tells us that the Olmecs were the dominant culture there from 1200 BC to 200 BC,[50] so they would have overlapped with Lehi's descendants for several hundred years. The Zapotecs established themselves in 600 BC and declined around AD 800, so they would have also been neighbors of the Book of Mormon people as well. The extensive Mayan civilization ran from around 1000 BC to AD 1700,[51] which easily encompasses the timeline of the Book of Mormon. Millions of Mayan descendants still live in Mesoamerica today.

Atlas of World Population History approximates that there were about 150,000 people living in Central America in 600 BC, when Lehi and his family landed in Central America.[52] Lehi's family had a total head count of about 50 individuals at that time. Thus, they made up about 0.03% of the Central American population, a percentage that cannot be considered significant.

Large civilizations had already been built when Lehi and his family arrived. *Archeology Magazine* has reported the discovery of a Mayan ceremonial platform, almost one mile long and up to 50 feet tall. It was found in Tabasco, Mexico near the Guatemala border. This places the platform right in the middle of Book of Mormon territory. It was constructed between 1000 BC and 800 BC.[53] This made the structure at least 200 years old by the time Lehi's family landed in the New World. There are hundreds of other such archeology finds in Central America, witnessing to the many inhabitants who were not related to the children of Lehi. Recognizing the fact that Lehi and his family made up a small minority in their Book of Mormon lands should not be interpreted as a concession. It's just a historical fact, supported by archeology finds and DNA sequencing research.

Let's return to the question of whether Lehi's family could have passed their Near East DNA sequences on to present-day indigenous peoples of Mesoamerica. If Lehi's family made up a very small proportion of Mesoamericans, it is much less likely their DNA would have been successfully passed on. Beyond just being diluted out by surrounding peoples, there are several historical events in Mesoamerica that would have reduced the likelihood that Lehi's and Ishmael's genetics were passed on. These events, called "population bottlenecks," are worth reviewing.

To define our terms, we read in the Gospel Topic Essay,

> A population bottleneck is the loss of genetic variation that occurs when a natural disaster, epidemic disease, massive war, or other calamity results in the death of a substantial part of a population. These events may severely reduce or totally eliminate certain genetic profiles.[54]

In other words, if a person born with a Jerusalem DNA sequence dies before having children, his or her sequence is lost forever. If enough people with that sequence die, then the Jerusalem DNA sequence can be lost entirely or become so rare as to be untraceable.

Did the Nephites and Lamanites lose people to natural disasters? Think of the many people who died from earthquakes, tsunamis, and other natural disasters that occurred just before the Savior arrived. Did the Nephites and Lamanites lose people to massive wars? Of course. Besides the dozens of "normal" battles related throughout the Book of Mormon that killed thousands, think for a moment about the final war in Mormon's own book in the Book of Mormon. The Nephite civilization was totally lost, and the Lamanite people were nearly destroyed as well. The bloodlines of the few survivors would have been severely diluted when integrated with surrounding peoples.

Did the Nephites and Lamanites lose people to diseases and epidemics? Indeed they did, but the most severe losses occurred well *after* the Book of Mormon timeline. After Columbus discovered America, the Spanish Empire expanded for four centuries (1492–1892) across most of present-day Central America, the Caribbean Islands, and Mexico. The European diseases they brought with them, such as smallpox, measles, typhus, and cholera decimated the indigenous peoples. For example, in Mexico, there were 25 million natives alive in the year AD 1500. By AD 1600 only one million Mexican natives lived—a loss of fully 96% of the starting population.[55] So, yes, there were several very severe population bottlenecks that we know about (and probably many that we don't). Such events would have been pivotal in eliminating the DNA sequences that Lehi and his family brought with him from Jerusalem.

With the understanding that few of the present-day indigenous peoples of Mesoamerica could be related to Lehi and Ismael, the charge that DNA evidence invalidates the Book of Mormon may be put to rest. The rebuttal of this charge was actually a good exercise in population dynamics for the Church. Not only was this attack on the Book of Mormon turned aside, we also learned a few facts that can be utilized in understanding this scripture.

What Have We Learned from DNA evidence?

As an aside, how does this discovery help us in our understanding of the Book of Mormon? Once you accept that the Book of Mormon peoples were a small minority in Mesoamerica, several questions about the scripture may be answered. For example, in Mosiah 25, we read,

> And there were not so many of the people of Nephi and of the people of Zarahemla as there were of the Lamanites; yea, they were not half so numerous. (Mosiah 25:3)

Well, how in the world did *that* happen? The Nephite and Lamanite groups were similar in size when they split up. Where did all these new Lamanites come from? Starting out at their arrival, if the Lamanites had gone out and incorporated small villages of Olmecs, Zapotecs, or Mayan into their ranks (either by force or negotiation) those additions would have made a big difference in their rate of population growth over the years. As their tribe grew larger, they could have incorporated even larger populations of surrounding peoples into their ranks. However, the Nephites would *not* have used force to recruit other populations. It was not their way. This difference in foreign policy between the two groups may explain their size disparities.

In conclusion, this science-based attack on The Church of Jesus Christ of Latter-day Saints initiated a rather major change in our understanding of the Book of Mormon. We should actually be grateful. However, if someone mentions that DNA sequencing proves the Book of Mormon false, remember that the peoples of the Book of Mormon did *not* make up a significant enough fraction of the indigenous peoples of the American continent for their DNA to show up regularly today. As you can see, the full explanation of the science is rather complex, but the summary of the fatal flaw of the criticism is not.

Chapter 14

Judging Church History—The Arrogance of Presentism

Presentism is defined as "the interpretation of past events in the light of present-day attitudes, rather than in the light of their own historical context."[56] In other words, every event in history must be interpreted in context of the values, practices, and beliefs of its time period. Historians regularly plead with their students not to judge historical figures by today's standards.

Nevertheless, few people seem to be listening to the historians as they judge world and Church history. The problem with judging history is that it often exposes more than a little hypocrisy in our judgments.

For example, critics of Joseph Smith point out that he was a treasure hunter. Indeed, Joseph was hired to seek for buried treasure.[57] We may scoff today, but in 1820 treasure hunting was rather popular. Joseph's family was not wealthy and took jobs where they could find them. What were the chances of Joseph finding buried treasure? About the same as the chance that a lottery ticket will pay off in the Powerball drawing tomorrow. In both cases, one is looking at a likelihood of success of less than one-in-a-million. Treasure hunting still goes on today—it just looks different.

Now, let's take a look at another peculiarity from the folklore of the days of Joseph Smith—seer stones.

Seer Stones

Folklore is, of course, the traditional beliefs, customs, and stories of a community, usually passed down by word of mouth. Many of these beliefs and customs are based on legends and lore.

Present-day mockers laugh at the idea that earlier generations believed in magic. We forget that in the mid-1800s science was just gaining some traction, mostly in Europe. Louis Pasteur had yet to develop milk pasteurization and vaccines for anthrax and rabies. X-rays had not yet been developed to diagnose a broken bone. The value of vitamins was yet to be realized. Jonas Salk would not develop a polio vaccine for 100 years.

Without science around to explain the reasons for disease, mental breakdowns, and strokes, oral tradition tried to fill in the gaps. Strange and ineffective remedies (such as bloodletting) were tried. Witching rods, also called dowsing or divining rods, were used to find underground water so that people of the time could dig their wells in the best place possible. Divining rods were also applied to finding treasure. There is no science behind the practice. No one would try it today, would they? Actually, if you would like to try water dowsing yourself, you can purchase your own dowsing rod on Amazon.com.

The fact that Joseph Smith used a seer stone to help him translate the Book of Mormon seems to bother a lot of people who are leaving the Church. It has become such a sticking point for people that entire books have been written about Joseph's seer stones. In the book *Joseph Smith's Seer Stones*, we read,

> Many who have criticized Joseph Smith's claims to be a prophet have made much of his use of seer stones. It has been all too easy to take advantage of the unfamiliar image of Joseph Smith translating the Book of Mormon while looking at his seer stone in the bottom of his hat.[58]

The assumption seems to be that Joseph, being a prophet of God, should have known better than to use seer stones. But why would that have been true? Why would one assume that Joseph Smith was so far ahead of his time to discern that folk magic didn't work? In all of Joseph's writings, I see no revelations from God explaining that his folklore practices were ineffective. I see no revelations that explain that milk pasteurization could save lives. Revelation doesn't work that way. Joseph knew only what he had been taught in his childhood. Again, taking from the book *Joseph Smith's Seer Stones*,

> For Joseph, Christianity worked together with folk religion, medicine, and common folklore. . . . Mormonism grew out of the Second Great Awakening, which embraced experiential religion and Christian revival.[59]

In our present day, we tend to look at folklore with patronizing skepticism. Who would believe in such nonsense, be it Joseph Smith or anyone else? We fail to perceive that we have our own folklore today. We believe what we are taught growing up. In actuality, we have so many of our own present-day myths, that we should be embarrassed to try to criticize past folklore. For example, many people believe that rock crystals have healing power, or that astrology can tell you what your day will be like. Others believe in the efficacy of unproven traditional Chinese medicines. The list of myths goes on and on. Today's medical folklore is a multi-billion dollar a year industry. If you go to your local pharmacy, you will find dozens of compounds with unproven medical claims lining the shelves. Folklore still exists and continues to have a powerful psychological effect on us.

Do Seer Stones Have Power?

The Urim and Thummim are described in the Old Testament as two stones that could be affixed to a breastplate (Exodus 28:30; Leviticus 8:8) for display. The stones were used as an aid to revelation. In 1 Samuel 28:6, we read about Saul, an Israelite king who was seeking for revelation.

> And when Saul inquired of the Lord, the Lord answered him not, neither by dreams, nor by Urim, nor by prophets.

Joseph Smith was given a Urim and Thummim by Moroni to aid in his translation. When Joseph first saw the two stones, he was probably not overly surprised at their appearance. By all appearances, the Urim and Thummim were two seer stones, mounted on silver bows to allow one to look through them. Joseph had seen seer stones before and even possessed a couple of his own. The Urim and Thummim were given to Joseph by Moroni with the golden plates—and almost assuredly confirmed Joseph's belief in the power of seer stones.

The Lord has a number of ways to give revelation. In the verse quoted above, Saul looked to his dreams, the Urim, and then to prophets for revelation. When those didn't work for him, he chose to visit a woman with a familiar spirit. We know that Joseph Smith wrote some of the sections of the Doctrine and Covenants using a seer stone. It appears that a seer stone can be an aid for the prophet as he receives inspiration. However, in later years Joseph did not need to rely on any help from a seer stone to receive revelation. Today, Church leaders in all parts of the world seek inspiration daily—and, as far as I know, none of them use a seer stone.

My own conclusion is that Joseph's seer stone did not have power in itself to help him to translate the Book of Mormon. Then again, I know nothing about the revelatory process required to translate ancient writings. How hard is it to do? There were times when Joseph wasn't in the right frame of mind to translate. Once he had argued with his wife Emma and was emotionally upset and unable to translate until the dispute had been resolved.[60] We read in Doctrine and Covenants section 9 that Oliver Cowdery tried to translate but was unsuccessful. The translation of the Book of Mormon was given by revelation. Though I may not believe in a stone with power to help in that translation, it is apparent that Joseph *did* believe in it. If the Urim and Thummim or a single seer stone placed in a hat helped Joseph to be more confident in his ability to receive revelation, then who am I to deny him that?

The arrogance of presentism does not allow us to consider how historical leaders were affected by the beliefs of friends, family, and society at large. Labelling the New England folklore of the 1800s as ridiculous and unseemly behavior for a church prophet may seem very progressive today. But our own society has little room to judge, as we still have our own folklore—in an age when we have the science to debunk faulty beliefs. Perhaps critics should be a little less judgmental of the folklore of past centuries.

Was Brigham Young a Racist?

This question is another favorite of our younger generation members who are leaving the Church. The whole issue of blacks and the priesthood has been a continued subject of unrest in the Church for a long time. I understand that racial sensitivity is running very high within our society today, but that doesn't change what happened in our history.

Brigham made the announcement that Blacks would not receive the priesthood in 1852. The Civil War would not start for another nine years. There were many people in the North working to end slavery. However, no one was working to end racism. The civil war and slavery would end in 1865, but division of whites and blacks continued. Black people had to use separate restrooms. They weren't allowed to vote. When city buses were introduced, Black people had to ride in the back.

This situation continued for *112 years!* The Civil Rights Act of 1964 finally outlawed discrimination based on race, color, religion, or gender. The Voting Rights Act of 1965 assured that Blacks could legally vote. The civil rights movement had gone on for about a decade by the time these two laws were passed. It is apparent that Americans only adopted anti-racist practices slowly and grudgingly.

Was Brigham Young a racist? The short answer to this question is yes, Brother Brigham was racially biased. He was the person responsible for deciding that Blacks in the Church should not receive the priesthood. However, the serpent side of our brain demands that we look at the assumptions behind the question and see if they are fair. In this case, there is a follow-up question that must be asked.

Was anyone in 1852 *not* a racist?

For Brigham Young to have *not* been racially biased, he would have been over a *century* ahead of his time. He wasn't, but no one else appears to have been either. In my reading of history, I haven't found the name of any public official or celebrity who stepped forward to demand the end of racial bias in 1852 or for many decades later.

As argued earlier in this chapter, the arrogance of presentism may allow us to think that, if *we* had lived in 1852, *we* would have passionately campaigned for the end of racism. While the northern half of the United States was willing to end slavery, neither half was willing to end racial bias for over a century. That is the historical backdrop that we must realize was in place at the time of Brigham Young's decision.

Why Did the Priesthood Ban Stay in Place for So Long?

It does not appear that Brigham Young ever claimed that he had a revelation from God regarding the ban of the priesthood from Blacks of African descent. President Young announced the policy change in the Utah Legislature instead of at general conference. This seems to indicate that he probably considered the announcement an administrative act and not a new revelation.

Now many may imagine that, after President Young's death, the Lord should have wanted to correct the mistake as soon as possible. However, once again we are putting our own earthly expectations upon the Lord, which He warns us not to do. Obviously, Church leadership wanted the ban to be lifted. For over a century, public relations were continuously damaged. Missionary work all over the world, especially in Africa, was significantly hindered. The prophets waited impatiently for a revelation.

Was the Lord chastising the Church for establishing the ban in the first place? Was there another gospel principle at work? Did the Lord simply not see this as a priority issue? We don't know. In the true Church of Jesus Christ, one should expect to find policies or revelations that don't make sense to the general public or even to Church membership. Should it surprise us that Jesus Christ might command policies in the Church—or allow them to continue—that are illogical to us? The Church teetered on the brink of extinction due to polygamy. Couldn't the Lord have commanded that it end sooner? The Church suffered slurs and public criticisms for decades for keeping the priesthood ban in place. Couldn't the Lord have terminated it sooner? If the Church was run exclusively by men and women, why would they make decisions that so significantly hurt its growth? However, in a church directed by God, one must expect that some church decisions will appear illogical. As Isaiah explained, "For my thoughts are not your thoughts . . ." (Isaiah 55:8).

The ban was finally lifted in 1978 by President Spencer W. Kimball. The Church had been praying for this moment for decades. I was on my Church mission in Mexico City when the ban ended. The public announcement came out on a Saturday. This was in the day before cell phones, so at first the announcement appeared to be a rumor. There was a faithful and active Black family in the ward to which I was assigned. Early Sunday morning, before sacrament meeting, the priesthood was given to this man and his two sons. The whole ward showed up to witness the ordinations. There were lots of hugs and handshakes and a celebration afterwards. I later heard that there were a few Church members who lamented the change, but the vast majority of the Church was thrilled.

Chapter 15

Defending Church History—Scriptural Translation via Revelation

IF YOU ARE READING THIS BOOK, THEN YOU REALIZE THAT THE WORDS WE choose are important. Consequently, I would like to clear something up about a word used extensively—and interpreted wrongly—within The Church of Jesus Christ of Latter-day Saints. The first, best- known definition of the word "translate" is to "restate (words) from one language into another language."[61] Thus, if you know English and Spanish, you can translate a Spanish document into English. Because the word "translate" has been used to describe how Joseph Smith wrote the Book of Mormon and the Book of Abraham, many people believe that Joseph read Egyptian words from the plates or papyrus respectively and then dictated their English translation to a scribe. This mental image is understandable, as there are a couple of well-known paintings of Joseph Smith gazing at the Book of Mormon plates as he translated them.

The word "translate" is not at fault for this confusion. The word has a second meaning, allowing it to be used in a broader context. From Vocabulary.com, we read,

> *Translate* comes from the Latin word *translates*, which means "carry across." The word isn't limited to talking about language. You can translate sales into dollars, or a play into a movie. When used that way, *translate* means changing something from one form to another.[62]

Notice this second definition of the verb "translate" more accurately describes what Joseph actually did. Through revelation from God, Joseph "carried across" the meaning of the reformed Egyptian written on metal plates to English written on paper. God translated the Egyptian to English and then revealed that English to Joseph.

The Book of Mormon

Much has been made about the process that Joseph Smith used to translate the Book of Mormon. Church members have had the image of Joseph Smith *reading* the golden plates etched in their minds from their days in Primary. Then we have an alternate image of Joseph gazing at a seer stone in the bottom of a hat, which we already discussed in the last chapter. In some way, Joseph's seer stone aided him in receiving revelation. But it was only an aid. As Joseph became more adept at receiving revelation, he stopped using seer stones and the Urim and Thummim altogether.

The Church has never taught that Joseph ever learned the written, reformed Egyptian language that was used by Book of Mormon writers. First, reformed Egyptian had been a dead language for centuries before Joseph's time. Secondly, the Church has never taught that Joseph needed to look at the plates as he "translated." The Lord did not need Joseph to be looking at a hieroglyph to give him the English words that it represented. The Lord could just relay the text to Joseph. It seems readily apparent that Joseph Smith never really *needed* to look at the plates themselves at all.

In the end, the plates were simply a physical manifestation to Joseph that the Book of Mormon really did exist. There was a reason that Mormon and the Nephite prophets before him had been commanded to keep a record. The existence of the plates offered proof to Joseph and his supporters that the record being translated was real.

The Book of Abraham

This same confusion about the meaning of the word "translate" occurs in discussions about the Book of Abraham. The Book of Mormon was completed in 1829; Joseph began compiling the Book of Abraham in 1835. In those intervening six years, Joseph Smith did *not* learn how to read Egyptian, reformed or otherwise. Classes in translating Egyptian hieroglyphs were not available at a local community college. Like the Book of Mormon, the Book of Abraham was received by revelation, not by Joseph Smith's capability in reading Egyptian.

In fact, in discussing the Book of Abraham, we must judge the book, not the scribe. As noted by Hugh Nibley in his book *Abraham in Egypt*,

> Joseph Smith is no longer with us; his reputation must rest on the bona fides of the book, *not* the other way around. By his own insistence, he was merely an implement in bringing forth the record, not its creator.[63]

In other words, attacks on the Book of Abraham by casting doubt on Joseph Smith and his ability to "translate" Egyptian is a hopeless strategy. Joseph Smith is dead, and we won't learn anymore about his linguistic abilities or his honesty by arguing about it further. Dr. Nibley's assertion is correct that the Book of Abraham must stand on its own merits. This is not a simple assessment; the Book of Abraham has a complex history. To understand both the criticisms and defenses of this book of scripture, a quick overview of its origins seems needed.

The Origins of the Book of Abraham

The Gospel Topics Essay written about the Book of Abraham is entitled, the "Translation and Historicity of the Book of Abraham." The following quotes are taken from this document.

> In the summer of 1835, an entrepreneur named Michael Chandler arrived at Church headquarters in Kirtland, Ohio, with four mummies and multiple scrolls of papyrus. Chandler found a ready audience. Due partly to the exploits of the French emperor Napoleon, the antiquities unearthed in the catacombs of Egypt had created a fascination across the Western world. Chandler capitalized on this interest by touring with ancient Egyptian artifacts and charging visitors a fee to see them. . . .
>
> By the time the collection arrived in Kirtland, all but four mummies and several papyrus scrolls had already been sold. A group of Latter-day Saints in Kirtland purchased the remaining artifacts for the Church. After Joseph Smith examined the papyri and commenced "the translation of some of the characters or hieroglyphics," his history recounts, "much to our joy [we] found that one of the rolls contained the writings of Abraham."[64]

Joseph's identification of the source of these writings is confirmed today in the Introduction to the book of Abraham. We read,

> The writings of Abraham while he was in Egypt, called the Book of Abraham, written by his own hand upon papyrus.[65]

From an initial reading of these two statements, one might think that the Church believes that Abraham physically wrote upon the very papyrus that Joseph Smith held in his hands. This misinterpretation, from those within or outside of the Church, is certainly not the general understanding today. As Hugh Nibley explained, the title of the Book of Abraham is actually, *The Book of Abraham, written by his own hand upon papyrus*." He goes on to explain,

> This is important, since much misunderstanding has arisen from the assumption that the Joseph Smith Papyri were the original draft of Abraham's book, his very own handiwork.[66]

Dr. Nibley goes on to explain that when a document written upon papyrus got too old and fragile, the ancient Egyptians copied it word-for-word to preserve the writing exactly as it had been written. Joseph had a copy of the writings of Abraham as well. From the title, it is apparent that Abraham wanted readers to understand that this document was an *autobiography* of his life—not a biography written by another author in the first person. In any case, Abraham assuredly did not write upon any of the fragments purchased from Michael Chandler.

Now, to continue with the history of the mummies and papyri. When Joseph Smith was martyred, his mother, Lucy Mack Smith inherited the artifacts. When Lucy passed away in 1856, Emma Smith obtained them. Emma quickly sold them to a man named Abel Combs, who sold most of the papyri and two mummies to the St. Louis Museum. When the St. Louis Museum closed in 1863, they sold the antiquities collection to the Col. Wood Museum in Chicago. In 1871, that museum and its displays burned to the ground in the Great Chicago Fire.

However, as mentioned, Abel Combs had kept some of the papyri for himself. He had mounted a few of the fragments and given them to his housekeeper. Her descendants later sold them to the Metropolitan Museum of Art in New York City. In 1967, The Church of Jesus Christ of Latter-day Saints purchased the papyri from the museum.[67] It was as if a piece of history had appeared out of nowhere. Both defenders and critics of Joseph Smith and his translation abilities were anxious to compare the Book of Abraham with the hieroglyphs of the recovered papyri to see if Joseph had translated it correctly.

As it turned out, eyewitnesses of Joseph working with the papyri testified that he had found the writings of Abraham on what they called the "long roll" of papyrus which had burned up in the Great Chicago Fire. The most significant fragment in the reduced collection of papyri contained the drawing that is now Facsimile No. 1 in the Book of Abraham. What little text surrounded Facsimile No. 1 was translated and found to be "a fairly common Egyptian funerary document called the Book of Breathings . . .."[68]

Over the years since Joseph's translation, critics of the Church have presented photos of the papyri fragments to teams of Egyptologists. One of the most famous of these evaluations was run by Francis Spaulding, an Episcopal bishop in Utah.[69] These Egyptologists did not find the Book of Abraham in the papyri fragments. Their publicized judgments were that Joseph's translation of the Book of Abraham was a hoax. Once again, however, these critics answered the wrong question. The Latter-day Saint faith has understood for many years that Joseph could not read Egyptian and had no idea how to translate hieroglyphs. The Book of Abraham was received by revelation, as was the Book of Mormon. In fact, the Egyptian papyri served much the same purpose as the Book of Mormon plates. They were physical proof of the existence and history of the scripture being revealed, enabling Joseph to understand them better and be inspired to translate them.

To respond to someone questioning you about the Book of Abraham, you might want to save yourself some time and ask, "Do you believe that scripture can be received by revelation?" If not, there is really no purpose in continuing the discussion. Joseph could not read or translate Egyptian—reformed or otherwise. The Church makes no claims that he did.

Joseph's Hobby

On a side note, Joseph Smith did have a hobby related to Egyptian hieroglyphs that may have contributed to this confusion. It is apparent that Joseph enjoyed studying ancient and foreign languages. Joseph worked on the translation of the Book of Abraham from July to November of 1835. In December, he interrupted that work when the opportunity arose to be instructed in Hebrew by a visiting Jewish scholar. (He was not able to return to his work on the Book of Abraham until March 1842, over six years later.) Joseph studied Greek and, later in his life, he studied German. It is important to note that Joseph's hobby was a separate activity from his day job of writing scripture through revelation. For example, during their work on the Book of Abraham, Joseph Smith, Oliver Cowdery, and W. W. Phelps created their own study guides to help them to better understand Egyptian. This assortment of documents is called the Kirtland Egyptian Papers. It includes copies of Egyptian hieroglyphs, drawings, a couple of papyrus fragments, early drafts of pages of the Book of Abraham, and a small book they also wrote entitled the *Grammar and Alphabet of the Egyptian Language.* However, there were major gaps and errors in these documents, and they would have been of little use in accomplishing an accurate translation. Hugh Nibley, who had a hand in organizing the documents, said of the source of the Book of Abraham,

> It is generally agreed that it could not have come from that papyrus called the Book of Breathings, nor can it possibly be the product of the clumsy and quickly abandoned gropings of the so-called Alphabet and Grammar. The Kirtland Egyptian Papers show us where it did *not* come from, and that is all.[70]

There are other instances where Joseph revealed an enthusiasm for his hobby. In April 1843, a group of men uncovered some bones and metal plates from an Indian mound in Kinderhook, Illinois. The plates were taken to Nauvoo to show to Joseph Smith. Joseph kept the plates in his home for a few days and made efforts to translate them with help from his Kirtland Egyptian Papers. Later, Joseph showed his work to others, including a correspondent from the *New York Herald* newspaper. He pointed out the similarities of some of the symbols on the plates to symbols in his study guide *Grammar and Alphabet of the Egyptian Language.* From his interpretation of one hieroglyph at the top of one of the plates, Joseph concluded that the plates were the history of a descendent of a Pharaoh. Other than that, Joseph never offered up a translation of the plates, and appeared to lose interest in them. It turned out to be a good decision on his part. In 1879, members of the group who discovered the Kinderhook plates revealed that they were a hoax. They had fashioned the plates to look like ancient records of a by-gone people.[71]

The story of the Kinderhook plates is still recited as proof that Joseph Smith was not a true prophet. Yet again, this conclusion is based on the mistaken belief that a prophet receives inspiration every minute of every day and, thus, can never be wrong. In his activities as an amateur hobbyist of ancient languages, Joseph Smith made errors. What amateur hobbyist doesn't? But this should not affect our judgments of Joseph Smith as a prophet of God.

Abraham in Egypt

Before we leave this fascinating and complex discussion topic, we should again consider the statement by Hugh Nibley that the Book of Abraham should be able to stand up on its own as an authoritative text. How would we go about doing this? Please allow me to quote from Nibley's *Abraham in Egypt* one more time.

> When any text is put forward as the genuine production of an ancient author of a given time and place, it remains only to compare the writing with documents known to be authentic coming from the same time and place and to weigh the points of conflict or agreement among them.[72]

Dr. Nibley wrote a fully indexed, 705-page book called *Abraham in Egypt* to meet his own challenge. His explanations are well-researched and exhaustively referenced. If you wish to understand this subject in greater detail, *Abraham in Egypt* is a must read. Dr. Nibley compares The Book of Abraham to other ancient texts that have come to light long since Joseph Smith was martyred.[73] He makes special note of the *Apocalypse of Abraham,* an ancient document preserved in Old Slavonic texts, which follows the narration of the Book of Abraham.

Naturally, there is different wording, but the story lines are nearly identical. For fourteen pages, Nibley runs side-by-side comparisons of the two books. Here are just the first two comparative verses.

> *Apocalypse of Abraham* IV—Hear my father Terah . . . how shall they [your idols] help you or bless me? And when he heard my words, he was very angry with me because I had spoken hard words against his gods.
>
> Abraham 1:5. My fathers, having turned . . . unto the worshiping of the gods of the heathen, utterly refused to hearken to my voice. Abraham 1:7. They turned their hearts to the sacrifice . . . unto these dumb idols, and hearkened not unto my voice.[74]

A companion piece called the *Testament of Abraham* was found, which also contains more such similarities. Abraham was an important person in Pharoah's court. It appears that other poets and authors of the time also recorded his history and teachings. Several such references are cited and described by Dr. Nibley. The Book of Abraham is not alone in its descriptions of Abraham's adventures in Egypt. As stated earlier, some of the attacks upon Church history require an understanding of the background of the debate. Translation of scriptures via revelation is certainly one of those topics. Other questions about Church doctrine require a precise understanding of what our doctrine really is—as we will discuss in the next chapter.

Chapter 16

Defining Church Doctrine

THE TERM "CHURCH DOCTRINE" CAN BE A FUZZY CONCEPT. MANY CHURCH members mistakenly believe anything ever taught at general conference is doctrine. That is not true. To be effective defenders of the faith, we need to know the definitions, or what Church doctrine is and what it is not.

The best definition I have read of the term "Church doctrine" is the following quote by Robert L. Millet. Please notice his repeated use of the word "today."

> In determining whether something is a part of the doctrine of the Church, we might ask, Is it found within the four standard works? Within official declarations or proclamations? Is it discussed in general conference or other official gatherings by general Church leaders today? Is it found in the general handbooks or approved curriculum of the Church today? If it meets at least one of these criteria, we can feel secure and appropriate about teaching it.[75]

Doctrine changes due to new revelation, societal pressures, scientific advances, and changing times. Many members defend their beliefs by quoting early Church leaders, when Church doctrine has actually moved beyond those declarations.

The talks given or books written by general authorities besides the sitting prophet and president of the Church are not to be considered Church doctrine. In fact, books written by such general authorities must include a disclaimer at the front of the book that reads something like, "The views expressed in this book are the responsibility of the author and is not an official publication of The Church of Jesus Christ of Latter-day Saints." Even the Bible Dictionary, which may be found between the Bible and the Book of Mormon in most triple combinations, is not to be taken as Church doctrine. In its preface we read of the Dictionary, "It is not intended as an official or revealed endorsement by the Church of the doctrinal, historical, cultural, and other matters set forth."

I think President J. Reuben Clark best explained how talks by general authorities should be understood. As he introduced a talk to religious educators in 1954, he declared,

> I am not declaring scripture, though I think I am not unscriptural. I am not declaring Church doctrine, though I think what I suggest is not contrary to Church doctrine. I have no right or authority to declare either scripture or Church doctrine. I will ask you to pay particular attention to these disclaimers. Please keep them always in mind in connection with what I shall say this morning.[76]

Ironically then, Bruce R. McConkie's well-known book *Mormon Doctrine* is not necessarily "Mormon doctrine." A controversial talk given at general conference by a general authority that makes headlines in the newspapers the next day is not to be considered Church doctrine either.

The Church has established doctrine as described above, but it also allows flexibility of beliefs. People are individuals who interpret gospel teachings differently. My own beliefs have been refined over the years, thanks to Church talks that give me different perspectives on various doctrines. I keep the perspectives and understandings that make the most sense and can stand up against argument. I discard those too weak to make the cut. This process is part of my growth and makes up much of my education. I appreciate hearing different perspectives, even when I don't agree with them.

However, if a Church authority in general conference teaches a doctrine from an extremely conservative or liberal viewpoint, critics gleefully declare those teachings to be Church doctrine. Church members who accept the assumption that all Church talks must be defended as Church doctrine will often find those discussions to be difficult. You can't win those arguments, because you don't have the same point of view as the Church authority you are defending. Thus, if you find yourself defending the specific words of an apostle or other Church authority, then pause to reconsider. Ask yourself if you are really debating a Church doctrine—or someone else's opinion about a Church doctrine.

It should not surprise anyone that The Church of Jesus Christ of Latter-day Saints has a wide range of beliefs within its membership. All other worldwide churches, be they Christian or not, contain their own wide ranges of belief structures as well. Admittedly, the Latter-day Saint temple recommend interview sets a minimum expectation of those members who wish to attend the temple. But, as a worldwide church, our political stances, lifestyles, religious observances, and gospel interpretations vary widely. In regard to social issues and doctrine, we shouldn't try to defend the specific opinions of other members, even if they are general authorities.

Being the prophet and president of the Church must be exhausting. The prophet presides at *every* Church meeting he attends. He most assuredly has multiple meetings every day that require making major decisions to ensure the health of the Church and its membership. But the prophet carries one more mantle that even the apostles don't carry—the responsibility to receive and communicate the doctrine of the Church. Though he may have mistitled his book, Elder Bruce R. McConkie understood that concept and explained it well.

> There is no question about receiving revelation for the Church; about announcing revelation for the Church; about expanding altering, changing, or modifying, in any way, any existing revelation or doctrine—all this rests with the President of the Church, who is the senior apostle of God on earth and the prophet, seer, and revelator who presides over and governs all others.[77]

In conclusion, "though I think what I suggest is not contrary to Church doctrine," my explanations in this book are not Church doctrine. Just because a topic is discussed by general authorities or Latter-day Saint writers, their conclusions are not Church doctrine either. That is . . . unless that general authority is the prophet and president of the Church. His words, when spoken as a prophet, may be taken as Church doctrine. This unique authority helps make his talks in Church meetings significantly more interesting.

Chapter 17

Woman's Suffrage

THE GOSPEL TOPIC ESSAY ENTITLED "JOSEPH SMITH'S TEACHINGS ABOUT Priesthood, Temple, and Women" was written to address the complaints by certain members of the Church that women are treated like second-class citizens. The Essay attempts to demonstrate that men and women share the responsibilities of priesthood power and service, which is true of course. But the explanation in the Essay does not address the complaint that women should be able to hold the priesthood.

This criticism does not accept the principle of the division of roles and responsibilities in a family unit. It assumes that men's and women's roles on Earth are the same. In fact, some who accept this assumption now claim that gender is a social construct choice, not a biological fact. This assumption ignores so many facts of life that the arguments that rest upon it lose any semblance of reason.

First, please understand that I am not arguing that it is the natural order of things that men go to work and women stay at home, barefoot and pregnant. If a father wants to be a stay-at-home dad and his wife wants to work full time in the business world, then so be it. The roles of "income provider" and "childcare provider" can be switched, or equally shared if both parents are working. But there are other roles of men and women that cannot so easily be exchanged.

The first role that cannot be exchanged is entirely biological. Men cannot get pregnant and bear children. At this point in the argument, women suffragists may say, "Well, of course they can't!" and try to move on to another topic in the women's rights debate. But let's look at this reality for a moment. Bearing children is critical to the survival of mankind, so the human body spends a lot of its time and energy on reproduction. Women's hormones control their monthly menstrual cycles, pregnancy, and the birth of their children. These powerful hormones affect a woman for most of her adult life. Likewise, only women can suckle babies, which, as mothers have told me, is another potential bonding event for mother and child.

Since so much of a woman's body is dedicated to reproduction, we might expect a woman's mind to be somewhat focused on it too. Everyone knows the meaning of the phrase "maternal instinct." The phrase communicates the love, protectiveness, and nurturing attitude of a mother. Whether it be due to the female hormones or how the female brain is wired, women are more emotional, more caring, and more nurturing—not only toward their own children but to others as well. Sorry dads, but when your child skins a knee and comes inside the house crying, that child is probably looking for Mom, not you.

The earthly professions of men and women were originally established due to their physical differences. Men are built to be stronger than women. This was important in the days when men had to protect their families and villages from the attacks of marauders. Strength was also critical in days not-so-long-ago when labor outside the home, such as farming, construction, and mining, was more manual and required physical strength.

Today we live in a world of machines and automation. Farmers no longer need to maneuver a horse and a heavy plow to plant their crops. They drive tractors, which can be done just as easily by a woman as by a man. Soldiers no longer fight with heavy swords and shields. They shoot guns, which can also be done just as effectively by women as by men. Advancements in our society have allowed women to move into roles they could not previously perform. As a society, we have struggled to accept this new reality, yet the transition is being made. However, new opportunities for women allowed by technology do not apply to the Lord's kingdom.

In the Old Testament, the tribe of Levi was tasked with the responsibility of carrying out the rituals of the Levitical priesthood. There is no record that the other eleven tribes were jealous of this assignment. This priesthood responsibility of the tribe of Levi was simply considered a part of the normal division of labor within Israel, much as it is today in the Church and the family.

The Lord has never indicated in any scripture that he wishes His daughters to hold the priesthood. It is a doctrine that has existed since the days of Adam. But I don't think God will make that change—in this life anyway. The roles and responsibilities of Motherhood are too important. To put this in perspective, when I depart this world, the only legacy I shall leave behind is my children. While I helped where I could, my wife Cheri is responsible for the majority of our success in raising those children. I have always held the priesthood in our family, but that responsibility pales in comparison to that of the role of mother provided by my wife.

There is more than a little irony in the argument about who gets to hold the priesthood. You see, I believe the Lord loves His sons . . . but He cherishes His daughters. First, I draw this opinion from the scriptures, the warnings of Jacob being the most descriptive.

> And I will not suffer, saith the Lord of Hosts, that the cries of the fair daughters of this people . . . shall come up to me against the men of my people . . .
>
> For they shall not lead away captive the daughters of my people because of their tenderness, save I shall visit them with a sore curse, even unto destruction . . . (Jacob 2:32–33).

My second reason is more personal. I have learned a lot about life from being a father of two sons and two daughters. If someone was to be dismissive or disrespectful to my sons, I would step back to let them deal with it themselves and to learn to be brave men. However, I found my love for my daughters includes a healthy dose of being overprotective of them. If I was to see someone offend a daughter or granddaughter, I believe I could quite easily resort to violence.

Most fathers would. I think God shares that overprotective tendency. How can anyone *not* cherish his daughters? My conclusion is that men who mistreat women are going to experience an *extremely* disappointing final judgment. But I digress. Let's get back to the discussion about the priesthood.

When the Genie in the Disney movie *Aladdin* appears from out of his lamp, he described the good parts and bad parts of a genie's life. He bellowed, "Phenomenal Cosmic Powers" and then in a high squeaky voice said, "Itty Bitty Living Space."[78] The point the Genie made in this statement was that all power comes with limitations. When we talk about the priesthood, we like to think of it as a "Phenomenal Cosmic Power." In this life, however, our actual priesthood power is very limited, a fact we can confirm by comparing our abilities with those of Jesus Christ while He was on Earth. The Savior could touch a cripple, healing him immediately. I can give a blessing to a cripple and, realistically, hope the Lord gives him some small comfort.

Sisters, though you may have grown up thinking the priesthood was a cosmic power—it's not. Not yet at least. Our serpent side encourages us to be brutely honest with ourselves in regards to our roles on Earth. In earth life, the priesthood is mostly a set of responsibilities and the authority to meet them. Each office of the Aaronic Priesthood has its own list of duties, as does each office in the Melchizedek Priesthood. A good explanation of the priesthood on Earth is that we are learning to handle guns safely by practicing with BB guns. We would *like* to be given a more powerful priesthood—or gun—but earth life is for learning, and we can only be trusted with BB guns here. When you have learned to use the BB gun safely, after this earth life is over, you can be trusted to handle larger guns, or more priesthood power. When priesthood holders have learned how to use authority without exercising unrighteous dominion, they will be trusted with greater authority and power.

When we are finally allowed to exercise significant power, there is every indication that women will have the opportunity to be priestesses in the next life. We hear in the temple that women will be ordained to be priestesses. Parley P. Pratt stated,

> It was from him [Joseph Smith] that I learned that the highest dignity of womanhood was to stand as a queen and priestess to her husband, and to reign for ever and ever as the queen mother of her numerous and still increasing offspring.[79]

Consequently, I believe women will be able to hold the priesthood in the next life. That priesthood will still contain a list of tasks and responsibilities. However, those tasks will require more authority and power to accomplish them, which will be provided. For now, we have so little information. But I think that, in the next life, men and women will be ordained with power as they become responsible enough to wield it.

To conclude, men and women are not the same biologically, mentally, or emotionally. There is an important message in that difference. Each gender is given talents to meet the expectations of earth life. It is fairly obvious that the Lord needs His daughters to be the chief nurturers and caregivers for their families and others. The Lord needs His sons to accomplish different chores, which occasionally require the priesthood. It is a simple division of labor, for which we are given the proper tools to accomplish.

Chapter 18

Plural Marriage—Asking the Wrong Question

For decades, most of the non-Latter-day Saint population in the world only knew three things about The Church of Jesus Christ of Latter-day Saints—and its name wasn't even one of them. No, most of the outside world only knew that Mormons were based in Utah, they attended college at Brigham Young University (BYU), and they believed in polygamy. Granted, some knew that polygamy was no longer being practiced, but the Manifesto ending plural marriage in 1890 was not really that well publicized.

Church members like to consider themselves a peculiar people, but it was polygamy that made us so in the eyes of the world. It is a doctrine that almost led to the destruction of the Church in the 1880s and it has haunted our missionary efforts ever since then. The Lord demanded its restoration, as we will discuss, and He probably knew what it would cost His church in the end. The Gospel Topics Essays actually dedicates *four* essays to the subject, recognizing the need to explain the doctrine as thoroughly as possible. The Church has endured much criticism around plural marriage. So, it only seems right that this book dedicates a chapter to it.

Many of the arguments discussed in earlier chapters have been applied to attacks on the Church regarding plural marriage. For example, the emotional argument has certainly been a favorite. ("Can you believe the Mormons believe in polygamy?!") The anecdotal evidence attack has also been used in the stories of disgruntled women who were once in polygamous marriages.[80]

To my female readers, I realize that this topic may generate anxiety, jealousy, and anger. Why would the Lord have ever approved of the practice of polygamy? What was the reason God felt that polygamy was a principle that deserved to be restored with all the other doctrines of the Restoration? How could God be so chauvinistic? Polygamy is such a controversial subject that many faithful members of the Church struggle with it still.

To their credit, the Gospel Topics Essays on plural marriage do a good job of reviewing the history of polygamy from its beginnings in Kirtland through the First Manifesto (September 1890) and the Second Manifesto (April 1904). But rehearsing of the history of polygamy does little to refute the assumption that polygamy was a mistake instituted by Church leaders more for lustful purposes than restoration. This is a complex topic and the questions about it must be worded correctly to get to the heart of the matter.

The question, "Did Joseph Smith receive revelation to reinstitute polygamy, or did he dream it up on his own?" is the wrong question for one simple reason.

No one living today has ever met Joseph Smith. No one has heard him speak or even seen a YouTube video of his talks. No one living has ever looked him in the eyes. We can read about him. But the reports available about Joseph vary wildly depending on the writer. To fairly judge the man today is impossible. To debate whether Joseph Smith received inspiration to restore polygamy is hopeless. How can we assess the righteousness, sanity, or deviousness of a man we have never met? We could judge Joseph from his actions as a leader of the Church. Yet, however much his critics disparage Joseph Smith, his actions were consistent with those of a man who believed he had spoken with God and was leading the Lord's church the best way that he could. The idea that we can somehow develop new insights into whether Joseph Smith received inspiration almost 200 years ago is nonsense.

The question we need to ask (and one that we might actually be able to answer) is, "Was plural marriage a gospel principle ordained by God that He insisted be restored with other truths in the latter days?" The judgment of the man Joseph is impossible, but a judgment of the *doctrine* of plural marriage is feasible.

The History of Plural Marriage—Sarah

From Adam's statement, "Therefore shall a man leave his father and his mother, and shall cleave unto his wife: and they shall be one flesh," it is believed that Adam and Eve were married.

However, we also hear about polygamy very early in the scriptures. Even before the birth of Seth to Adam and Eve, we learn about Lamech, a near descendent of Cain, who took two wives named Adah and Zillah. Most of us should probably admit that we cannot really imagine the life that women led in 2000 BC. But a few Old Testament stories might help us to better understand their situation.

In Genesis 21, Sarah, the wife of Abraham, thinks she hears Hagar, the mother of Abraham's son Ishmael, mocking her. Between this and her worry that Ishmael may compete with Isaac as heir, Sarah tells Abraham to get rid of the woman.

> Wherefore she said unto Abraham, Cast out this bondwoman and her son: for the son of this bondwoman shall not be heir with my son, even with Isaac. (Genesis 21: 10)

Please note that Sarah calls Hagar a bondwoman, essentially a slave. Hagar was not Abraham's wife, so she didn't have the rights of a wife. The fact that Sarah can tell Abraham to throw Hagar out of the camp—and probably to her death—may give you some insight into the situation women faced in ancient days. In verse 11, we learn that Abraham was grieved to have to cast out his son Ishmael! We read,

> And the thing was very grievous in Abraham's sight because of his son. (Genesis 21:11)

The Lord does tell Abraham that Hagar and Ishmael would be preserved, and that Ishmael's descendants would become a great nation. That information probably helped Abraham to feel a little less guilty about the eviction. But Abraham does as his wife requests.

> And Abraham rose up early in the morning, and took bread, and a bottle of water, and gave it unto Hagar, putting it on her shoulder, and the child, and sent her away: and she departed . . . (Genesis 21:14)

When the water is all gone, Hagar places Ishmael under a bush and walks away because she doesn't want to see him die. Many Christians turn away from the barbarism of this story, but we need to face the facts of ancient times. In most ancient societies, women had no rights. They could be bought and sold. A single woman with no man to care for her was especially vulnerable. The prophet Abraham was simply following societal norms of his time. As we all know, the Lord saved Hagar and a great nation arose through her son Ishmael.

Now let's consider the story of Ruth.

The History of Plural Marriage—Ruth

In the book of Ruth, the narration tells us that Ruth's husband and his brother die, leaving Ruth and her mother-in-law Naomi without support. Ruth has nowhere to go and begs Naomi to be permitted to go with her. They go to Bethlehem, where they glean barley and wheat from the remnants left after the harvesters have been through the field. This was a form of welfare in these ancient days, established by the Mosaic Law, to provide for people who had no other source of food (Leviticus 19:9–10). It was grueling work to collect a little grain. But that was the best deal that Ruth and Naomi could find.

Boaz, the owner of the grain fields, sees Ruth in the fields and gives her some attention and grain. Ruth indicates her interest in Boaz and sleeps at his feet one night. Boaz buys a plot of land owned by Naomi's husband and sons—and with the transaction Ruth is purchased to be his wife!

> And Boaz said unto the elders, and unto all the people, Ye are witnesses this day, that I have bought all that was Elimelech's, and all that was Chilion's and Mahlon's, of the hand of Naomi.
>
> Moreover Ruth the Moabitess, the wife of Mahlon, have I purchased to *be my wife* . . . (Ruth 4:9–10, italics added)

Please note that this was a happy ending for Ruth! She became Boaz's wife and would no longer have to glean remnants from grain fields. There is no indication if Boaz had a first wife or not.

We read that he does not consider himself to be a young man (Ruth 3:10), and he is reported to be a man of wealth. There is no reason to believe that Boaz was a bachelor. The writer of the book of Ruth did not deem it important enough to mention if Boaz had a first wife or not.

These two stories illustrate the plight of women in ancient days. It was an extremely hard life. Women did not own land. Women working away from the home was not only discouraged—it was nonexistent. There were no government welfare programs. It was a day and age that if a woman was offended by her husband and walked away from her home—she could starve to death or die of exposure.

Especially during wars, which were plentiful in ancient days, there were usually more women than men in the land. It was a dangerous time. Besides war casualties, men died from defending their homes and livestock from robbers and wild beasts. Granted, many women died in childbirth, but often men had the shorter life expectancy. If a childless woman died from the plague, her husband would continue his job and find a new wife. If a childless man died from the plague, his wife had the one option of returning to live with her family—if any of them still lived.

Why Polygamy?

So, in ancient days, what do you do with an excess of widows who have no one to support them? What do you do with their young children? Where do they go if they don't have a male relative to care for them? There were no women's shelters or soup kitchens. There were no jobs for single women. Women working outside of the home wouldn't occur for a few thousand years.

Women could, of course, be kept as concubines. But the kept woman would have no legal claim that her man care for her. Should the man die, a concubine would have no rights to receive an inheritance for her or the children she had by him. Enter the practice of polygamy.

Some of the great men of the Old Testament, held up as examples of righteousness and obedience to the Lord, came from polygamous families. Abraham had two wives. Isaac had four wives, from which the twelve tribes of Israel arose.

A man named Elkanah had two wives, Peninnah, who had children, and Hannah, and who had no children. Hannah went to the prophet Eli for a blessing, which he gave her. It came to pass that Hannah conceived and bare a son, called Samuel, who became a prophet. In the book of Judges, we read of the righteous king of Israel called Gideon who had threescore and ten sons, *for he had many wives.* Abijah was a righteous king of Judah, whose life was chronicled in 2 Chronicles.

In chapter 13, we read that "Abijah waxed mighty, and married fourteen wives, and begat twenty and two sons, and sixteen daughters."

What is noticeable in all of these Old Testament references is the tone of the reports that great prophets and kings had multiple wives. There is no negative judgment at all, no suggestion that these men had done anything wrong. Polygamy was an established and accepted part of the culture.

The Rights of Wives

The Mosaic Law included laws regarding women's rights that were very progressive for their day. In the following Old Testament scripture, note that Israelite wives were given rights that non-Israelite women of the time did not share.

> If she please not her master, who hath betrothed her to himself, then shall he let her be redeemed: to sell her unto a strange nation he shall have no power, seeing he hath dealt deceitfully with her.

> And if he have betrothed her unto his son, he shall deal with her after the manner of daughters.
>
> If he take him another wife; her food, her raiment, and her duty of marriage, shall he not diminish. (Exodus 21:8–10)

In other words, if a man took a second wife, the rights of his first wife would remain intact. In Deuteronomy 21:15 we read about how the rights of the firstborn stay with the firstborn, even if he is born to a less favored wife. In Deuteronomy 25:5, we read:

> If brethren dwell together, and one of them die, and have no child, the wife of the dead shall not marry without unto a stranger: her husband's brother shall go in unto her, and take her to him to wife, and perform the duty of an husband's brother unto her.

From this verse and the story of Ruth, we learn that, when a man died, the immediate family or a kinsmen had the responsibility of marrying and caring for his widow. As an aside, this was the Mosaic Law that the Sadducees based their "What If" question to the Savior, trying to both trap Him and prove there was no resurrection. "What if," they asked, "a man with six brothers married a woman and then died without having had children. She marries the second brother who also dies, so the third, fourth, fifth, and sixth brothers all marry her and die as well. Who would she be married to in the resurrection?" (Mark 12:18–25). Please note that the surviving six brothers were all probably married, since Jewish men were usually married between the ages of 18 and 20.[81] But the fact that the new widow would be a plural wife was apparently not noteworthy enough to mention in the Sadducees' question. Polygamy was still quite common in Jesus's time and marrying your brother's widow was still standard practice.

If the man marries a wife, or a second wife, or a third, he has legal responsibility to care for all of them. She has a right to receive sustenance and support, and later an inheritance. Polygamy was the most practical way to care for widowed women and orphans. The woman would be legally married to the man of the house. There would be no danger of breaking the law of chastity or that living arrangements might appear to be inappropriate. The woman would be cared for and, for her part, carry out responsibilities of the household.

The Muslim religion incorporated plural marriage into their beliefs as well. The Koran of the Islam religion ordains that a Muslim can marry up to four wives, but only if he can care for them all equally well. Again, a key of their doctrine is to care for dissociated women. The Prophet Muhammad married several of his twelve wives because they were war widows.[82]

Polygamy also gave women more choices in their lives. Consider the following fictional explanation, which may illustrate this idea. Let's say there was a small remote village where lived 100 single women and 100 single men. As pairings usually go, the prettiest girl married the best provider in the village. The marriages continue, as the girls pick out, court, and marry men who are good providers. Eventually, we come down to the last five single women, who have to choose between the five *poorest providers* in the village. These last five men are lazy, drunk, dirty, and possibly abusive. Does it make more sense for these last five women to marry these five bottom-of-the-barrel men—or for them to seek to be second wives of one of the better providers in the village? Granted, second wives did not have the privileges of first wives. But then again, they would not have to live in poverty and squalor. How would you choose? What would you wish for these five women?

Thus, for the first 4,000 years of Earth's history, polygamy was a means for the societies of men to take care of God's daughters. *That* was the original principle behind polygamy. As a father of two daughters, I understand this concept. A father wants his sons to go out and conquer the world. But he wants his daughters to be protected, even in ancient societies that did not value women.

Bearing Children

Besides taking care of single women, widows, and orphans, there was another reason for polygamy—to bear children. If you remember, Sarah only sent Hagar into Abraham's tent when she decided she could bear no children of her own. In the book of Jacob, the Lord reinforces this second reason for polygamy. We read in Jacob 2,

> Wherefore, my brethren, hear me, and hearken to the word of the Lord: For there shall not any man among you have save it be one wife; and concubines he shall have none. . . .
>
> For *if I will*, saith the Lord of Hosts, *raise up seed unto me*, I will command my people; otherwise they shall hearken unto these things. (Jacob 2:27, 30; italics added)

If the Lord needs a particular people to grow in numbers, He will command it. We may not be comfortable with that reason, but some of that inability is due to our modern way of thinking. We are used to being surrounded by millions of people. The thought that an entire people could be extinguished from the earth is unthinkable. However, in ancient days, entire civilizations disappeared from history. In the Americas, for example, the Olmecs, Anasazi, and even Mayan civilizations were lost. In the scriptures, we read of the demise of Ten Lost Tribes of Israel and the Nephites. In view of such a possibility, if the Lord rises up a people that He doesn't want to lose, He reserves the right to command polygamy (Jacob 2:30).

As civilizations developed, and widows and orphans could be better cared for by the government, the practice of polygamy was discontinued. Therefore, monogamy first became law in the two earliest centers of civilization—Athens and Rome. It spread from there, helped significantly by the support of the Roman Catholic Church. Between AD 600–900, monogamy became the established norm for marriages throughout Europe.[83]

Today polygamy is still practiced in areas across Africa and in parts of Asia. However, it is practiced mostly as a symbol of the husband's wealth in countries where a big family means increased status.

The point of this chapter is that plural marriage was first instituted in the days of Adam and was kept in place for about 4,500 years. During that time, it saved countless single women, widows, and orphans from destitution and starvation. Nowhere in the Bible is polygamy criticized or frowned upon. It was an option that was associated with eternal marriage, to be implemented at the command of the Lord. To fully restore the temple covenants of marriage and eternal families, polygamy also had to be restored.

Restoration of *All* Things

We tend to think of the Restoration as only restoring familiar church doctrine, such as baptism by immersion (Matthew 3:16), having a prophet and twelve apostles (Matthew 19:28; Ephesians 4:11), having bishops (Titus 1:7), the Aaronic and Melchizedek Priesthoods (Hebrews 5:1–4; 7:11, 12), and sending out missionaries two-by-two (Luke 10:1). Indeed, these doctrines and callings *were* all part of the Restoration. But the Restoration included much more than just basic gospel doctrines.

A restoration was predicted because of the falling away, or apostasy, that was prophesized to occur. In his second letter to the Thessalonians, Paul assured them that the Second Coming was not imminent, as a falling away needed to occur first.

> Let no man deceive you by any means: for that day shall not come, except there come a falling away first, and that man of sin be revealed, the son of perdition. (2 Thessalonians 2:3)

Then, in his letter to the Ephesians, Paul spoke of the restoration of all things by our Heavenly Father,

> That in the dispensation of the fulness of times he might gather together in one all things in Christ, both which are in heaven, and which are on earth; even in him: (Ephesians 1: 10)

In the book of Acts, we find Peter crying repentance to an audience that had gathered on Solomon's Porch in Jerusalem. Peter reminds them that he represented Jesus Christ and then gives them an update as to where the Savior was.

> And he shall send Jesus Christ, which before was preached unto you:
>
> Whom the heaven must receive *until the times of restitution of all things*, which God hath spoken by the mouth of all his holy prophets since the world began. (Acts 3:20–21, italics added)

This restoration, still occurring even today, encompasses many gospel principles. It also includes world-famous events, such as the restoration of Israel to its place. In May 1948, the United Nations officially established the independent nation of Israel. David Ben-Gurion, then head of the Jewish Agency, was established as its first prime minister. People of the Jewish faith have been gathered and restored to their proper place.

A Restoration is Requisite

Perhaps because it was a fairly recent event in religious history and only a small portion of the world recognizes it, the Restoration has not been assigned the importance that it deserves. It is a major event in Christianity—and it had to be done properly. We read in the 41st chapter of Alma.

> I say unto thee, my son, that the plan of restoration is *requisite* with the justice of God; for it is *requisite* that all things should be restored to their proper order. (Alma 41:2, italics added)

The declaration that there must be a restoration of all things is repeated throughout the scriptures. Even if the principle being restored is out of date, such as the commandment to Christians to forgo the worship of graven images, it was restored. Even if the principle being restored was decidedly unpopular, like polygamy, it had to be restored. The original principle behind the practice of plural marriage, to protect and care for the daughters of God, is still valid—even if the people of modern times dislike the ancient solutions.

Plural marriage was not the party that many people think it was. Polygamy was difficult for the Saints. The law estranged husbands and their first wives. Many members left the Church, outraged at the new doctrine. Polygamy brought about increased persecution—from both mobs and the federal government. Church leaders were imprisoned or had to flee to Mexico. Emma Smith, wife of Joseph, was especially hostile to the principle. As summarized in the Gospel Topics Essay on plural marriage,

> This principle was among the most challenging aspects of the Restoration—for Joseph personally and for other Church members. Plural marriage tested faith and provoked controversy and opposition. Few Latter-day Saints initially welcomed the restoration of a biblical practice entirely foreign to their sensibilities.[84]

Though we have never met him, would Joseph Smith have chosen to bring increased oppression, member desertions, and government action against the fledgling church? Would he have voluntarily imposed such challenge and discord into his own marriage? There can be little argument that Joseph did not handle the reintroduction of polygamy very well. He kept the news from Emma, his brother Hyrum, and other Saints. Trying to keep the truth of polygamy within a small circle of Church members, yet meet the Lord's command to restore it, led to rumors and accusations, both within the Church and outside of it.

Thus, polygamy really was a lose/lose situation for the prophet Joseph. He was commanded to restore the ordinance of plural marriage, a practice that was considered deplorable by modern society. Yet we should remember that plural marriage was once a practice that provided for the welfare of women. It was once a part of the Mosaic Law. The scriptures promised a restitution of *all* things, not just the popular doctrines of the time. Polygamy was part of the complex doctrine of eternal marriage. It, too, had to be restored, despite the many difficulties it imposed on the Church.

To conclude, the question regarding modern-day plural marriage is not whether Joseph Smith was a true prophet or a con artist. We cannot answer that question. We can, however, review the history of plural marriage and recognize that, for most all of human history, it was an accepted option of the marriage covenant. As such, it was included in the Restoration.

Chapter 19

Temples, Covenants, and Masons

There are significant similarities between the restoration of temple ordinances and the restoration of plural marriage. The Lord did not choose to be patient in restoring either doctrine, and the commandments to do so came at very difficult times for the Church. The command to build a temple in Kirtland Ohio was received in June 1833 (D&C 95:11). The Church had to take out significant loans just to buy the land for the temple. Throughout its entire construction, the Church struggled financially with building costs. During the absence of men during the Camp of Israel, women and children worked on the job site.

In August 1833, just *two months* after the command to build a temple in Kirtland, the Lord commanded His people to build another temple in Independence, Missouri.

> Verily I say unto you, that it is my will that a house should be built unto me in the land of Zion, like unto the pattern which I have given you.
>
> Yea, let it be built speedily, by the tithing of my people.
>
> Behold, this is the tithing and the sacrifice which I, the Lord, require at their hands, that there may be a house built unto me for the salvation of Zion— (D&C 97:10–12)

In the introduction of this section of the Doctrine and Covenants, we read, "Members of the Church in Missouri were at this time subjected to severe persecution, and on July 23, 1833, had been forced to sign an agreement to leave Jackson County." The Lord seemed determined to build a temple in Missouri, though a casual observer would have deemed it impossible. Lands were purchased in December, but due to financial difficulties and continued persecution, the temple was never constructed.[85]

The Kirtland temple was dedicated in March 1836. By the beginning of 1838, excommunicated dissenters had seized the building for their own church meetings. Threats of mob violence and warrants for Joseph's arrest continued. Finally, on January 12, Joseph Smith and Sidney Rigdon and their families left Kirtland. They would soon be followed by the rest of the remaining faithful Saints.[86] Three years in construction, the Kirtland temple only functioned as a temple for about half of that time.

In April 1838, the Lord commanded that a temple be built in Far West, Missouri (D&C 115:8–9). The massacre at Hawn's Mill, less than twenty miles away, took place six months later, in October. Some excavation work had been accomplished on the site, but construction was never initiated.

The Saints fled from Missouri to Commerce, Illinois which Joseph Smith renamed Nauvoo. In January 1841, the Lord commanded the Church to build a temple there (D&C 124:27). However, following the same unfortunate series of events, persecution of the Saints mounted. On June 27, 1844, Joseph and Hyrum Smith were executed in Carthage jail. In January 1845, the state of Illinois repealed Nauvoo's city charter. From the book *Saints*, volume 1, we read,

> Without these protections, Brigham feared, the Saints would be vulnerable to attacks from their enemies. Yet the temple was far from finished . . .. But staying in Nauvoo, if for only another year, could put everyone's lives at risk.
>
> Brigham went to his knees and prayed to know what the Saints should do. The Lord responded with a simple answer: stay and finish the temple.[87]

By December, the temple was complete enough that the attic could be dedicated for the performance of temple endowments. For the next two months, members crowded the temple to take out their endowments and be sealed as families. On February 4, 1846, several hundred Saints received their temple endowments even as the first wagons rolled out of Nauvoo towards the west.[88] On May 1, the completed temple was dedicated, but no more temple work would ever be carried out there. Immediately after the ceremonies, furnishings were removed, and the temple was evacuated.

Once the Saints entered Utah, the frantic pace of temple building slowed down a bit. Brigham Young entered the Salt Lake Valley on July 24, 1847, a date still commemorated in the state as "Pioneer Day." In April 1877, fully thirty years after their arrival, the St. George temple was dedicated, making it the first functioning temple in the state. On April 6, 1893, President Wilford Woodruff dedicated the Salt Lake City temple.

Today, Latter-day Saint temples still draw skeptical interest from the world. It seems many people don't like being told they are not permitted to enter a church building. They wonder what we do in temples that needs to be so secret. The Church has always responded that temple activities are not secret, but sacred. After construction, but before its dedication, the Church holds open houses so that non-members may tour the temples. During those tours, the basics of the temple ordinances are explained. Nonetheless, suspicions of secret rituals still exist, and we should be prepared to respond to them. To do so, we should understand something about temples of the Old and New Testaments.

The Holy Place and the Most Holy Place

From the days when Moses led the Children of Israel out of Egypt, we read about temples. While Israel was still wandering in the wilderness, the first temple was actually more of a tent, called a tabernacle. It was dismantled and carried when Israel needed to change locations. God gave to Moses very specific instructions as to the size of the tabernacle, its furniture, decorations, and even arrangement (Exodus 25–27). There were only two rooms in the tabernacle. The outer compartment was called the Holy Place. It contained an altar for incense, a candlestick with six branches, and a table upon which the shewbread was placed. Only the priests of the temple could enter this room.

The inner compartment was an even *more* holy place and was called, quite logically, the Most Holy Place or the Holy of Holies. This room only contained the Ark of the Covenant, within which were the two tablets of stone, etched with the ten commandments that Moses brought down from the top of Mount Sinai. The lid of the Ark was called the Mercy Seat. It had a gold- covered cherubim on each end. The two cherubim faced one another, and their wings converged to form a cover over the Mercy Seat. Only Moses and the high priest were allowed to enter. In Exodus 25:22, we read God's instructions to Moses about the Holy of Holies,

> And there I will meet with thee, and I will commune with thee from above the mercy seat, from between the two cherubims which are upon the ark of the testimony, of all things which I will give thee in commandment unto the children of Israel.

This same design was copied in the construction of Solomon's Temple in Jerusalem, and then continued in both Zerubabel's restored temple and then Herod's Temple. Holy places, with restricted access and dedicated for only the most sacred of ordinances, have been in temples since the days of Moses.

Jesus's Defense of the Temple

Was the temple important to Jesus Christ? Yes, this is an easy conclusion to make from the scriptures. As discussed previously, Jesus Christ was usually very calm, humble, and dovelike. However, there were a couple of times in the New Testament when the Savior put aside His calm and humble attitude. In fact, He got extremely angry over the desecration of the temple in Jerusalem—not once but twice. In John 2, we read,

> And the Jews' passover was at hand, and Jesus went up to Jerusalem,
>
> And found in the temple those that sold oxen and sheep and doves, and the changers of money sitting:
>
> And when he had made a scourge of small cords, he drove them all out of the temple, and the sheep, and the oxen; and poured out the changers' money, and overthrew the tables;
>
> And said unto them that sold doves, Take these things hence; make not my Father's house an house of merchandise.
>
> And his disciples remembered that it was written, The zeal of thine house hath eaten me up. (John 2:13–17)

Oxen, sheep, and doves were being sold to be offered as sacrifices. The moneychangers were there to convert foreign coin into local currencies, so that purchases could be made and the temple tax paid. It was rather like a large convenience store had been set up in a corner of the temple—and the Savior took offense.

It is believed that Jesus's eviction of moneychangers and animal auctioneers occurred in the Court of Women. Though it was certainly not the Holy of Holies, the Court of Women was still contained within the temple walls.

Three years later, Jesus was again in Jerusalem to celebrate Passover. During this visit He would suffer the Atonement, be arrested, be crucified, and be resurrected. But before all that occurred, He took time to return to the temple—and clear it out a second time. We read in Mark 11:15–17,

> And they come to Jerusalem: and Jesus went into the temple, and began to cast out them that sold and bought in the temple, and overthrew the tables of the moneychangers, and the seats of them that sold doves;

> And would not suffer that any man should carry any vessel through the temple.
>
> And he taught, saying unto them, Is it not written, My house shall be called of all nations the house of prayer? but ye have made it a den of thieves.

Besides clearing out the merchants working on the temple grounds, Jesus also stopped men from carrying vessels through the temple grounds. The temple was hallowed ground, not a sidewalk people could take as a shortcut. There is an interesting difference between the two cleansings observed by James Talmage in *Jesus the Christ*,

> On the former occasion, before He had declared or even confessed His Messiahship, He had designated the temple as "My Father's house"; now that He had openly avowed Himself to be the Christ, He called it "My house."[89]

Twice, the Savior testified to the sacredness of the temple in surprising acts of anger and indignation. His people had forgotten that the temple was a holy and sacred place, dedicated to temple sacrifices and the teaching of the people. From the portable tabernacle of Moses in 1440 BC to the destruction of Herod's temple by the Romans in AD 70, the children of Israel had a temple for about 1,500 years. It is clear from the scriptural accounts in the New Testament that the Savior revered the temple and considered it to be the House of the Lord.

Temples Since Christ's Atonement

With Christ's Atonement, the Mosaic Law was fulfilled and complete. However, most of the ordinances performed in the temples, such as animal sacrifices, were done to fulfill requirements of the Mosaic Law. For Christians, with Christ's Atonement accomplished, animal sacrifices and the need for Old Testament temples became a thing of the past. For Jews, temple rites continued until AD 70, when Herod's temple was destroyed by Romans under the command of general Gessius Florus.

The principle of consecrated, restricted-access buildings dedicated to completing sacred ordinances continues today. We still have temples, but the ordinances performed there have changed to be in accordance with the law of the gospel. The temples are still restricted access; only those who pass a temple recommend interview are allowed to enter. This principle of restricting access to holy places is well documented in the scriptures. We know it will continue in the afterlife. As explained in the New Testament, you must be judged to be righteous before you are allowed access to the kingdom of God.

> Jesus answered, Verily, verily, I say unto thee, Except a man be born of water and of the Spirit, he cannot enter into the kingdom of God. (John 3:5)

> Then said one unto him, Lord, are there few that be saved? And he said unto them, Strive to enter in at the strait gate: for many, I say unto you, will seek to enter in, and shall not be able. (Luke 13:23–24)

> It is easier for a camel to go through the eye of a needle, than for a rich man to enter into the kingdom of God. (Mark 10:25)

If someone ever questions you about the restrictiveness of temple admittance, you might point out that heaven will also turn away those who do not meet a certain standard. Besides being a place for ordinances, temples provide a sanctuary, separate from the rest of the world, where Church members can commune with their Heavenly Father.

The Covenants and Ordinances Have Changed

If you run a keyword search of the word "covenant" in the scriptures, you will find that the Old Testament contains the word 256 times. The New Testament contains the word only 23 times.

The Lord made a number of covenants with His people in the Old Testament, but they were almost all temporal promises. The Lord is very thorough in explaining this concept, as we read in Doctrine and Covenants.

> And verily I say unto you, that the conditions of this law are these: All covenants, contracts, bonds, obligations, oaths, vows, performances, connections, associations, or expectations, that are not made and entered into and sealed by the Holy Spirit of promise, of him who is anointed, both as well for time and for all eternity . . . are of no efficacy, virtue, or force in and after the resurrection from the dead; *for all contracts that are not made unto this end have an end when men are dead.* (D&C 132:7, italics added)

> Behold, I say unto you that all old covenants have I caused to be done away in this thing; and this is a new and an everlasting covenant, even that which was from the beginning. (D&C 22:1)

The Doctrine and Covenants contains the word "covenant" 92 times, most of which refer to the "new and everlasting covenant."

> For behold, I reveal unto you a new and an everlasting covenant; and if ye abide not that covenant, then are ye damned; for no one can reject this covenant and be permitted to enter into my glory. (D&C 132:4)

The new and everlasting covenant is actually made up of six or seven parts. It begins with baptism, then the gift of the Holy Ghost, and then receiving the priesthood—all of which may be completed in our chapels. However, then we must move our covenant-making into a temple, where we receive our initiatory covenants, the endowment, and sealing of spouses (or of a whole family). Put them all together and you have made the new and everlasting covenant. Each covenant has its own requirements as to what the covenant-maker must do.

Masonic Rituals

One of the stranger criticisms of Joseph Smith and temples is that there are parallels between the endowment temple ordinance and Freemasonry rites. This issue has been brought up enough that it was included in the Gospel Topics Essays. Indeed, there are probably some similarities. During the time that Joseph Smith was figuring out and teaching temple ordinances to other Church leaders, he did join the Masons. Perhaps a little history is in order.

On January 19, 1841, in Nauvoo, Joseph received Doctrine and Covenants section 124. Joseph and the Church were commanded to build a temple in Nauvoo. The Lord wished to reveal temple ordinances to His people, and a temple would be needed to complete them. We read,

> And verily I say unto you, let this house be built unto my name, that I may reveal mine ordinances therein unto my people;
>
> For I deign to reveal unto my church things which have been kept hid from before the foundation of the world, things that pertain to the dispensation of the fulness of times. (D&C 124:40–41)

From Church historian Richard Lyman Bushman, we read a little more of the background and history of the temple ordinances.

> In Kirtland, Joseph . . . performed the rituals of washing and anointing in the House of the Lord. In Nauvoo, the ceremonies were further elaborated to include baptism for the dead, endowments, and priesthood marriages.[90]

So, during the time of the Nauvoo temple construction, Joseph was figuring out what the Lord wanted regarding temple baptisms for the dead, endowment, and sealings.

There are certain church activities that the Lord requires us to do in very specific ways. A good example is the prayer offered over the bread and water of the sacrament each Sunday. The wording of the two prayers is given in Doctrine and Covenants section 20, in a revelation believed to have been received in 1830. Only one word has been changed in those prayers since their revelation. After Joseph received Doctrine and Covenants section 27 allowing him to replace wine with water in the sacrament, the word "wine" was replaced by "water." Otherwise, the sacrament prayer has not been changed since the Lord revealed it.

But temple ordinances are not like the sacrament prayer. Numerous changes have been made in the temple programs, especially in the initiatory ordinances and the endowment. The covenants themselves have not changed, but some of the wording and steps in taking out those covenants have been modified. It seems apparent that the Lord gave Joseph the covenants, certain wording, and actions that were to be included in His temple ordinances, but then let him put the final script together.

In January 1841, the Lord commanded Joseph Smith to build a temple in Nauvoo. Joseph worked on writing the script of the endowment ordinance to be performed there until his death in June 1844. Joseph did become a Mason during that interval, specifically in March 1842.

Did Joseph Smith Incorporate Masonic Principles into the Temple Endowment?

Given the overlap in the time that Joseph Smith was receiving inspiration and writing the temple endowment, there has been a long-running debate as to whether Joseph incorporated Freemasonry principles into the temple endowment. Several books have been written about the subject and the argument continues even today. Regarding this debate however, a serpent may ask the question, "Does it somehow matter if Joseph incorporated Masonic principles into the temple endowment?" Joseph had been commanded to develop a procedure and script for the temple endowment ceremony. If he discovered principles or wording in Freemasonry that helped him to accomplish his goals, why would he not use them? When creating a new book, a new structure, or a new work of art, doesn't everyone pull together bits and pieces of their experience and education and use them in the new design?

It appears that much of the initiatory and endowment ordinances authored by Joseph were fluid and changeable. This is evident since, over time, the Church has made many changes to the original ordinances to better teach temple concepts to a modern world. In conclusion, if someone asks if Joseph Smith incorporated Masonic rituals into the temple endowment, the best response is probably to respond that it is indeed possible that he did. There are quotes by early Church members that indicate they believed it was true.[91] However, there seems to be little need for argument. It is almost certain that Joseph used what he knew to create an endowment ordinance that told a story, taught gospel principles, and incorporated the making of covenants. If he used some of the wording or concepts from Masonic rituals to better communicate principles of the endowment, so much the better.

One Last Thing

We have a strong work ethic in The Church of Jesus Christ of Latter-day Saints. In fact, we even consider attending the temple as "doing our temple work," thus providing needed ordinances for our dead. This is a fine goal of course, but there should be more in attending the temple than accomplishing ordinances. After all, we have an eternity to accomplish those temple ordinances. They will get done.

So, during this earth life, while we are still working out our salvation, maybe we should focus more on the time given to us in the endowment room and the celestial room. There we can ponder our lives, rest, and maybe even experience a few spiritual moments. The work of accomplishing temple ordinances is important, but so is your testimony and peace of mind.

Especially in these latter days on Earth, let us remember to take the time to commune with God in His holy temple.

Chapter 20

Homosexuality and the Church

It is very easy to get into a debate about Latter-day Saint doctrine and homosexuality. There has been much public debate on the rights of the LGBTQ community, and much anguish at the scriptures that teach against its choice of lifestyle. It was nearly inevitable that the two organizations would come into conflict.

The Church of Jesus Christ of Latter-day Saints has made great effort to communicate to the world what should be a simple concept. The Church will gladly embrace homosexuals and welcome them into our congregations. However, the Lord's church cannot embrace the practice of homosexuality. That refusal makes some people angry. Such people identify so strongly with homosexuality that they consider anyone who rejects the lifestyle as rejecting them as individuals. They take personal offense, not because the Church has done something personally offensive, but because it will not accept their sexual lifestyle choice as something righteous and good.

Granted, numerous other Protestant churches have embraced and celebrate the gay lifestyle. However, The Church of Jesus Christ of Latter-day Saints has not. One of the main reasons for this refusal is that the Old Testament has a rather strict code of morality. We read,

> Thou shalt not lie with mankind, as with womankind: it is abomination. (Leviticus 18:22)

> If a man also lie with mankind, as he lieth with a woman, both of them have committed an abomination: they shall surely be put to death; their blood shall be upon them. (Leviticus 20:13)

But the verse quoted above from Leviticus 20 that forbids homosexuality is just one of a whole set of restrictions regarding sexual conduct. The chapter goes on to forbid a person having sex with . . .

- Verse 10—Another man's wife
- Verse 11—Your father's wife
- Verse 12—One's daughter-in-law
- Verse 13—Another man
- Verse 14—One's mother-in-law
- Verse 15—A man and a beast
- Verse 16—A woman and a beast
- Verse 17—A sister
- Verse 18—A woman during her period
- Verse 19—An aunt
- Verse 20—The wife of your uncle
- Verse 21—A sister-in-law

Many of these restrictions are repeated in Leviticus chapter 18. Some of these restrictions are based on the commandment to avoid incest, which is also forbidden (Leviticus 18:6). This list of restrictions makes up a moral code that was apparently quite important to the Lord. Many of these verses also identify the penalties for disobedience of these moral laws, most of which were death or being exiled. In Leviticus 20, the Lord summarizes the reasons for His moral code.

> Ye shall therefore keep all my statutes, and all my judgments, and do them: that the land, whither I bring you to dwell therein, spue you not out.
>
> And *ye shall not walk in the manners of the nation, which I cast out before you: for they committed all these things, and therefore I abhorred them.*
>
> But I have said unto you, Ye shall inherit their land, and I will give it unto you to possess it, a land that floweth with milk and honey: I am the Lord your God, which have separated you from other people. (Leviticus 20:22–24, italics added)

The tone of these verses in Leviticus is unequivocal. The Lord supported the Israelites in displacing the Canaanites who had lived in the Land of Promise. The inhabitants were not living the moral law. In Leviticus 18, we read,

> (For all these abominations have the men of the land done, which were before you, and the land is defiled;)
>
> That the land spue not you out also, when ye defile it, as it spued out the nations that were before you. (Leviticus 18:27–28)

Why sexual laws are so important to the Lord is a deeper philosophical debate than we can attempt here. But the Lord is very clear in His commandment. Consequently, despite the many demands upon the Church to rescind its stand on LGBTQ lifestyles, it will continue to follow the moral law.

The New Testament

I have heard the argument that a moral law may have been important in the Old Testament, but since the commandment is not mentioned in the New Testament, it was not important to the Savior. However, the Savior's teachings were designed to explain how His new gospel differed from the Mosaic Law. While animal sacrifice was discontinued, the basic commandments of the Old Testament were pretty much unchanged.

This fact is illustrated by the story of the rich young man. As we read in Matthew 19:16–19,

> And, behold, one came and said unto him, Good Master, what good thing shall I do, that I may have eternal life?
>
> And he said unto him, Why callest thou me good? there is none good but one, that is, God: but if thou wilt enter into life, keep the commandments.
>
> He saith unto him, Which? Jesus said, Thou shalt do no murder, Thou shalt not commit adultery, Thou shalt not steal, Thou shalt not bear false witness,
>
> Honour thy father and thy mother: and Thou shalt love thy neighbour as thyself.

In response to the rich young man's question of which commandments he should obey, the Savior listed off the sixth, seventh, eighth, ninth, and fifth of the Ten Commandments. He then refers to Leviticus 19:18 to "love thy neighbor as thyself." Obviously, Jesus Christ was simply referencing the Old Testament commandments, as if it was common understanding that Old Testament laws must still be followed.

During the Sermon on the Mount, the Savior indicated that if anything, the moral law commandments were now even *more* restrictive than the Mosaic Law had been. In Matthew 5, we read,

> Ye have heard that it was said by them of old time, Thou shalt not commit adultery:
>
> But I say unto you, That whosoever looketh on a woman to lust after her hath committed adultery with her already in his heart. (Matthew 5:27–28)

The Law of the Gospel demanded even more of its followers than the Mosaic Law. With it, we now must keep both our actions and our thoughts pure. The Lord has been explicit in His commandments around moral behavior, however unprogressive they may appear to younger generations.

Seeking Your "True & Natural Self"

As discussed earlier, words and their meanings are important. The phrase "natural impulse" requires some discussion. As explained by Ty Mansfield, an author and therapist for those with same-gender attraction,

> Even with same-sex attraction, some people manage it quite well despite the possible belief they'll never get married to someone of the opposite sex in this life, but others feel that it is simply too much of a load to bear and too unreasonable for the Church to require them to sacrifice their desires. There also seems to be this assumed idea that because a feeling or impulse or desire is "natural," it must also therefor be good or morally acceptable. "Natural" does not necessarily equate to good or desirable.[92]

In fact, rarely do impulses of the natural man translate into something good. Paul discussed the "natural man" in his letter to the Corinthians.

> But the *natural* man receiveth not the things of the Spirit of God: for they are foolishness unto him: neither can he know them, because they are spiritually discerned. (1 Corinthians 2:14, italics added)

Mosiah supports Paul's teaching in the third chapter of Mosiah in the Book of Mormon. One's soul must be strong enough to overcome the desires of the natural man.

> For the *natural* man is an enemy to God, and has been from the fall of Adam, and will be, forever and ever, unless he yields to the enticings of the Holy Spirit, and putteth off the natural man and becometh a saint through the atonement of Christ the Lord . . . (Mosiah 3:19, italics added)

It has become very fashionable for people to declare that they are seeking to "find their true selves" so they can "live their best lives." However, such quests often take the form of sorting through one's natural desires of the flesh and choosing which are the most exciting. Finding your true self is admittedly a lifelong task. Your natural man is a product of your genetics, your family, your upbringing, your education, your successes, and your failures. Your spiritual self includes the preexistent spirit that resides within you. The goal of finding your true self is to allow the two sides of you to merge, such that your natural man recognizes the joys of following its spiritual side and ceases to argue with it.

To summarize, The Church of Jesus Christ of Latter-day Saints is attempting to communicate to the world and the LGTBQ community that it welcomes those who battle homosexual attraction. However, it can never embrace the practice of homosexuality itself. The scriptures strongly forbid it, and the Church cannot sanction the concept of giving up the battle against sin and choosing to live the lifestyle of the natural man. In this regard, the Church and the homosexual community are at an impasse. There are no further reasons to criticize either side of the dispute.

If someone attacks the Church for its refusal to accept the homosexual lifestyle, the best strategy is to admit that the Church must continue in its refusal. Scriptures and other teachings of the gospel are contrary to the lifestyle, and the Church cannot accept those things which the Lord finds so deeply objectional.

Chapter 21

Underlying Assumptions and Truths

In the end, what is the point of all the criticisms and attacks upon the Church, especially regarding its history? Attacks on the decisions by Joseph Smith, polygamy, actions by Brigham Young, the Mountain Meadows massacre, not detecting Mark Hofmann's forgeries sooner, refusing the priesthood to Blacks, even foolish actions by young missionaries are repeatedly recounted because of one underlying—and incorrect—assumption.

That assumption being, if the Latter-day Saint faith represented the true Church of Jesus Christ, it would not make such mistakes. Its leaders would have been too inspired and its membership too loving and Christlike to have made such serious mistakes throughout Church history. If this were the Church of Jesus Christ, then Joseph Smith should have been a golden boy, untarnished with accusations of being a treasure seeker. Polygamy would never have been introduced into the church. Brigham Young would have never denied the priesthood to Blacks of African descent. The Mountain Meadows attack would never have occurred. Mark Hofmann would have never been able to fool two prophets and other Church leaders with his forgeries.

By such reasoning, the true church of the true God should be quite easy to find. We simply need to look for an error-free church with a snow-white history. First, we must find a church whose leaders are continuously inspired. The doctrines of this church would not offend today's social norms. Secondly, we just need to find a church whose members are truly Saint-like and never offend their neighbors, coworkers, or fellow church members.

Even speaking this underlying assumption out loud makes it sound ridiculous. Perfect churches with perfect members do not exist. God does not give uninterrupted revelation to anyone, including His prophets. People are people and people are messy. Religion teaches compassion and empathy to its members, and it succeeds up to a point. Yet, we have no angels in our congregations. I have never seen anyone translated. However, to be fair, I do know many faithful Church members who are working hard to accomplish those goals.

The Role of Religion

Now that we know the underlying assumption behind criticism of the Church, we might ask, "What is the underlying truth of attending church?" Indeed, why does anyone attend church? Obviously, people get along in life without religion. Tens of millions of people do it every day. If you wish to defend the practice of religion, we must ask, "What are these people missing?" There is, after all, a cost for every decision. If you sacrifice eating, you starve. If you sacrifice exercise, you become overweight and lethargic. What is the cost of sacrificing your religion?

Asked in another way, what are the advantages of attending church? There are a number of answers to this question, but we want to find the ultimate underlying truth. The answer may seem obvious, but I think it has been lost in the many debates about the existence of God and criticisms of doctrine.

Simply put, religion was established from the beginning *to help us to improve, to become better people.* Whether you see that as the evidence of a well-lived life or as the only way to attain the celestial kingdom, it is one and the same. One may argue that, no, religion was created by God so that we can worship Him. By this interpretation, God requires a great amount of admiration, compliments, praise and even flattery. That simply does not line up with my image of Heavenly Father. However, if one of the goals of worship is to recognize and express appreciation for our blessings, then worship does help us to become better people.

Others may object that religion was created to teach us faith and obedience. However, in the bigger picture, faith and obedience allow us to become better people. We have faith that our obedience to God will help us to become more knowledgeable, empathetic, capable, and spiritual people. The earth itself provides appreciable opportunities to become better people. We learn of trust and friendship in our youth. We learn resilience and courage as we work to feed and shelter ourselves. We learn patience and love from being spouses and parents. We learn empathy and appreciation as we become elderly.

However, earth life can only teach us so much—and it is not enough. Church and religion were designed to teach us other ways to improve ourselves and to prepare for the afterlife. We learn about the commandments to direct our behavior along the paths that God recommends. We learn about repentance, so that when we err, we know how to get our act together again and resume our learning. We are given church callings so we can learn the skill of interacting with other people. We tithe to learn obedience and charity. We attend church to be taught, reminded of the gospel plan, and encouraged to follow it. Much of our more advanced learning—in knowledge, emotional maturity, and love for others—occurs at church. You are on earth to move beyond childish selfishness and to evolve to become a higher being. You are here to follow a higher path and find wisdom and love. You need other people to counsel, teach, and encourage you in this process.

But You Can't See It

If you go to the gym to build up your strength and physique, there are several ways to track your progress. Upper arm diameter will tell you how your arms are developing. So will the number of curls you can do with a thirty-pound weight in your hands. If you are on a diet, body weight will tell you how you are doing. When dealing with our physical body, it is easy to measure our progress.

When trying to gauge the condition of your spiritual self, measurement is much more difficult. Has your church attendance, prayer, and obedience the past year had a beneficial effect on you? You can't really tell; there is no gauge or scale to measure spiritual accomplishment. For this reason, people stop attending church. They may stop believing in an afterlife. In any case, they don't see their progress towards it. If certain people can't measure how spiritual pursuits and church worship are helping them deal with life's challenges, they often simply become inactive.

Traditional Worship

In the 1970s, the religious community witnessed the buildup of so-called megachurches. These houses of worship broke all the stereotypes of small churches with ministers who preached fire and brimstone. Services at megachurches are still held in large, open buildings. Members can wear T-shirts and blue jeans to church services. Music is composed of upbeat compositions by bands with electric guitars and drums. Sermons are also upbeat but based on very general topics so as to not challenge the beliefs of anyone in the congregation. Many disillusioned members of The Church of Jesus

Christ of Latter-day Saints wonder why their church can't be more like that, basing their belief on the assumption that churches need to be progressive, not traditional.

Admittedly, Latter-day Saint church services have changed very little since April 1830, when the Church was organized. In fact, they have changed little since the days of the New Testament, when the original church was organized. We pray and sing traditional hymns. We listen to talks and sometimes get to hear special musical numbers. The chapels are simple in appearance. Men generally wear suits and women usually wear dresses. Yet the Church is not following traditional church services just because they're traditional. There are reasons behind every aspect of Sunday worship. Church dress helps us to remember to act respectfully. Church hymns are majestic, reverent, and aimed to put us in a mental and emotional state to best worship God. Talks and lessons are designed to teach us gospel principles and give us different perspectives on those teachings. Many decry the fact that The Church of Jesus Christ of Latter-day Saints is not as progressive as other religions—and it is not. But the Church does not seek to be progressive. Of greater importance is setting the proper tone for church services.

The wisdom of the serpent encourages us to look for the reasons behind what goes on around us. Why do others criticize the Latter-day Saint faith? What are the assumptions behind these attacks? On the other side of the coin, why are church services structured as they are? What is the underlying reason for church worship? To survive the challenges of present-day earth life, we must look beyond outward appearances to understand what we are doing and why we are here.

PART 3

Future Needs for a Serpent's Wisdom

Chapter 22

A Balance between Dove and Serpent

I MAY HAVE APPEARED SOMEWHAT HARD ON DOVELIKE ATTITUDES IN THIS book, so some clarification is probably in order. From my descriptions, I hope you have learned that serpents are honest with themselves and realistic about the world. They are cautious to the point of being suspicious about the intentions of others. They realize that life is hard for everyone—but even harder on the naïve and innocent. Serpents are wary and try to take notice of everything around them. They constantly seek for knowledge and wisdom, because they form the best defense against being caught unawares. They are rarely fooled by scams or those who would take advantage of one's charity.

On the other hand, we have the dove. The dove takes all the suspicions of the serpent—and puts them aside. The dove realizes that being a serpent is not necessarily a happy way to live. One should appreciate a friendly pat on the shoulder—and not be afraid the hand holds a knife. To learn from others, we must trust in them. To move forward in life, you can't always be turning around to check what's coming up from behind you.

Yet, being a dove in our day is not easy. When life is hard, many people lose their kindness, generosity, and concern for others. Paul was correct in his assessment of the latter days.

> This know also that in the last days perilous times shall come.
>
> For men shall be lovers of their own selves, covetous, boasters, proud, blasphemers, disobedient to parents, unthankful, unholy. (2 Timothy 3:1–2)

Not only will people stop trying to display the gentle attributes of the dove, they will despise and disparage those who do. Continuing to the very next verse in 2 Timothy, we read,

> Without natural affection, trucebreakers, false accusers, incontinent, fierce, *despisers of those that are good*, (2 Timothy 3:3, italics added)

And here is the problem. When we become world-weary from dealing with the difficulties of life, we often begin to focus only on ourselves. To your serpent side, this is a very logical move. If you are unhappy, you must change something to be happy again. An unhappy person often pushes away family and friends to focus on their own needs. They allow their frustration and emotions to silence their dove side, which wants to be more generous and giving.

So, we need to continually find a balance between the caution of the serpent and the goodwill of the dove. Let's look at how the balance manifests itself in a few aspects of life, both anciently and today.

The Mosaic Law versus the Gospel

In many respects, the serpent can be compared to the Mosaic Law. The adage "an eye for an eye, a tooth for a tooth" (Leviticus 24:20) is a simple reflection of the law of consequence. There is no better way to learn about, and survive, the dangers of earth life. If you know that a certain behavior will generate a specific penalty, you will modify your behavior to avoid that danger.

Small children must learn the Law of Consequence. If you touch fire, it hurts. If you hit your brother, he will hit back. Likewise, the Law of Consequence was a major feature of the Mosaic Law, a lower law designed to prepare the Children of Israel for the higher law of the gospel plan.

The dovelike characteristics in the Law of the Gospel introduced the concepts of repentance, mercy, forgiveness, and compassion. Forgiving someone is a divine act of compassion, voluntarily dismissing the penalty of someone else's poor behavior. Doves are to be harmless, humble, and willing to forgive. Nevertheless, the serpent cannot be forgotten; there still must always be a balance. For example, in Acts chapter 5, church members Ananias and Sapphira decided to hold back some of their donation to the church from the sale of some land. They lied to Peter, the prophet of the church, and thus to the Lord. It was a grievous sin, and they both died for that decision.

Even under the Law of the Gospel, there must still be consequences to bad behavior. Many people don't believe this. As discussed earlier, to the question, "What would Jesus do?" they believe the Savior would always choose the most dovelike response. On this earth at least, such a policy would lead to chaos. There must always be a balance of the justice of the Serpent and mercy of the Dove.

Forgiveness

Forgiveness only works if you can be dovelike. The serpent takes the attitude, "Fool me once, shame on you. Fool me twice, shame on me." If you have wronged someone, the serpent will conclude that the data is in, and you should not be trusted. When you ask someone to forgive you, you are asking them to forget their actions of the past. This is not a logical thing to do. A serpent is loath to do such a thing, but a dove will be forgiving.

This is another good example to better understand when your dove and serpent should have a meeting of the minds. How often must you forgive someone? Peter asked this question.

> Then came Peter to him, and said, Lord, how oft shall my brother sin against me, and I forgive him? till seven times?
>
> Jesus saith unto him, I say not unto thee, Until seven times: but, Until seventy times seven. (Matthew 18:21–22)

Peter asked if he should forgive seven times because seven represented completeness in the Old Testament. Peter wanted to know when he could be completely done with someone in his life who constantly required forgiveness.

But Jesus's response that we should plan on forgiving 490 times is a bit of an oversimplification. Forgiveness can be freely given—but trust cannot. Let's say you have a friend who borrows money from you, never repays those loans, and continually asks for your forgiveness. You have two questions that you must answer. First, do you forgive him? Second, do you continue lending him money? Forgiving does not mean being gullible or forgetful. Even the Lord won't do that (D&C 82:7). In regards to your freeloading friend, there is a point where you cross over from being generous to being foolish. Your serpent side and dove side must work together to figure out where that point is.

The Parable of the Good Samaritan

The parable of the good Samaritan is a good comparison of the concept of serpent and dove. To begin, we should recognize that the traveler who fell among thieves did a foolish thing. He fell among thieves while traveling alone from Jerusalem to Jericho. To make this trip, he had to pass through the Judean wilderness, where lone travelers were easy prey.[93] The man had been stripped of his clothes and left half dead on the deserted road. We may wish to chastise the priest and the Levite who saw the man and walked away—but they were just being cautious. The wounded man could have been a decoy for another band of thieves. How could they tell? It was much safer for them to not be delayed or burdened while on this dangerous road.

Had this not been a parable, when the good Samaritan stopped to help the wounded man, the serpent side of his brain would have been screaming at him to move on. Instead, the Samaritan set aside his fears and spent his time and money to help the wounded traveler. Jesus ended the parable with a question of the lawyer who had first requested a definition of his neighbor. Jesus said,

> Which now of these three, thinkest thou, was neighbour unto him that fell among the thieves?
>
> And he said, He that shewed mercy on him. Then said Jesus unto him, Go, and do thou likewise. (Luke 10:36–37)

The path of the dove is a higher path than that of the serpent. It includes showing mercy and kindness to those around you. It's also a riskier path. The Good Samaritan was lucky. The "wounded traveler" could have had a knife in his hand ready to stab the Samaritan when he knelt down to help him. It is left to each of us, when making a major decision, to realize your serpent side and your dove side must work out the risk/reward of any situation.

Raising Children

Raising one's children requires constantly balancing the promptings of the dove and the serpent. The dove encourages trust, but the serpent prioritizes caution. Thus, parents allow their youth to leave home during the day to socialize and have fun. But parents also set curfews, because everyone knows that "nothing good happens after midnight." The serpent is a parent's practical side. When a mother refuses to allow her daughter to wear immodest clothing, it is not because her child may get cold. It is because Mom knows what immodest clothing can communicate about a person, and she doesn't want that message to be sent about her little girl. Most parental limitations are based on life experiences and accumulated wisdom of the serpent. As a junior in high school, my daughter and her girlfriend wanted to spend the night in sleeping bags by the school "spirit rock" before the big football game. They wanted to protect it from being spray painted by the rival school. There was so much wrong with this plan, that my serpent-side refused to allow it.

It is the parent's dove side that must often calm their serpent-side and allow their children to learn to drive, leave for college, depart for missions, and even get married. The world-weary serpent side of parents will warn their children of all that can go wrong in the cruel world. Yet offspring leave the house anyway. When a parent has conflicting emotions about raising a child, it is generally because their serpent and dove sides are arguing about what is best. Recognizing this fact may help one understand the source of those emotions.

Food Storage

Having food storage is yet another good example of balancing the wisdom of the serpent and the generosity of the dove. A good food storage is a recognition that the worst things imaginable—be they earthquakes, war, anarchy, or social upheavals—can occur to disrupt our food supplies. The serpent recognizes these dangers and makes plans to survive them. Yet, if we are too much the serpent, we will lock ourselves away in our homes, with guns and ammunition at the ready to protect our food from others. As Church leaders have affirmed, the generosity of the dove must continue within us even in perilous times. If we still want to follow the Savior in the face of disaster, we must be ready to share our food and water with our neighbors.

Do Not Fear Listening to the Serpent

The Savior gave us an important nugget of wisdom when He told His missionaries to be as gentle and doves and as wise as serpents. In life, in church, in raising a family, we must constantly balance the two persuasions in our decisions. We shouldn't feel that we are not being Christlike when we must face the realities of life and make decisions that will not be popular with others. On the other hand, we shouldn't forget to be generous and caring when life gives us blessings that allow it. In Church services, members are taught to be dovelike much more than they are taught to be serpentlike. We must recognize the need for both attitudes in daily life and make our decisions accordingly.

One last note. During my years of Church service, there were two times that I had to become very serpentlike and tell my Church leaders that I could not continue in a calling. Business travel, job changes, personality conflicts, and other challenges had made burdens of those callings. The situation was affecting my testimony and my desire to attend church. I could not continue to allow my calling to be so detrimental to my faith. I will never regret those decisions. Church leaders cannot read minds and usually don't know what personal burdens their ward members are facing. At times, your best friend may be your serpent side encouraging you to rectify a bad situation to preserve both your testimony and activity in the Church.

Chapter 23

The Latter Days

Joseph Smith wrote an account of the First Vision which is now included in the Pearl of Great Price. To set the stage for his narration, he writes,

> Some time in the second year of our removal to Manchester, there was in the place where we lived an unusual excitement on the subject of religion. . . . Indeed the whole district of country seemed affected by it, and great multitudes united themselves to the different religious parties . . . (Joseph Smith—History 1: 5)

Joseph then goes on to describe how the excitement evolved to become contention between the religions, making it impossible for him to choose a religion based on their teachings. But, in hindsight, what an interesting time to have lived—when an entire region of the country knew enough about religion to be excited about it and to debate different doctrines! It has always been dangerous to discuss politics and religion. However, most Christians knew that even in debate they should try to remain Christlike. It was a day when Christians could have a dovelike attitude because very few people sought to eradicate their beliefs.

Today we don't live in such a religiously focused time. In fact, we live in a day and age when people know so little about religion that the traditional missionary door approach doesn't work anymore. Residents behind those doors have no common ground with the missionaries upon which to begin a discussion. Many people have heard about Jesus Christ only because He is associated with Christmas. As Church members, we may still seek to be good missionaries, but in doing so, we must be aware of the changes in the mission field. Christians can no longer be as doves, freely discussing gospel topics with work associates and neighbors. We must, instead, be aware that the religious faithful are a minority today. We must choose our words so as not to offend. Speaking about religion was common in 1820, but today it is rather unusual and, often, a much more uncomfortable conversation.

The Savior told His apostles to be as wise as serpents because *He wanted them to survive* their missions. They wouldn't be able to do that if they didn't recognize new threats and avoid the dangers behind them. He wants members of His church to do the same today. Unlike Joseph Smith, we don't need to worry about the Methodist's disputes with the Protestants. We must worry about the criticisms of those who disparage everything about God, religion, and obeying the commandments. Such critics have the grand stage of social media to declare their denouncements. Through podcasts, websites, and videos, critics are directing their skepticism, sarcasm, and general disgust with religion at anyone who will listen. Our two youngest generations, who read, listen, or view social media more than older adults, have been most affected by this attack.

The Church Will Diminish

The wisdom of the serpent requires that we all face reality, however grim the picture might be. On the one hand, the following analysis is depressing. Yet, the results are fairly conclusive—and it is better to prepare ourselves for inevitabilities than to ignore them. Worldwide, Church activity and membership is declining. A quote from a Gallup poll in the United States states,

> Church membership is strongly correlated with age, as 66% of traditionalists -- U.S. adults born before 1946 -- belong to a church, compared with 58% of baby boomers, 50% of those in Generation X and 36% of millennials. The limited data Gallup has on church membership among the portion of Generation Z that has reached adulthood are so far showing church membership rates similar to those for millennials.[94]

This report is in line with similar polls about religious observance from the Pew Research Center and the General Social Survey (GSS). Jana Riess, who wrote *The Next Mormons*, reports the same declines of religious belief in The Church of Jesus Christ of Latter-day Saints, as discussed in chapter 9.[95] Members of each generation are abandoning their religions, though for distinctly different reasons. The Silent Generation were born between 1928 and 1945. These elderly Latter-day Saints are leaving The Church of Jesus Christ of Latter-day Saints in greater numbers because they are passing away. While death is a good reason for leaving the earthly Church, it still reduces membership numbers. The Baby Boomer generation is a large generation, born between 1946 and 1964. Church members from this generation are also starting to leave the Church in increasing numbers as its oldest members pass away.

Generation X was born between 1965 and 1980. Theirs is a split generation, with some members following in the footsteps of their parents' beliefs and others adopting the more rebellious beliefs of their children. The infamous Millennial Generation was born between 1981 and 1995. Theirs has been a distinctly rebellious generation, as reflected by the numbers of their age group who are leaving Christian churches throughout the world.

Generation Z is our youngest adult generation, born between 1996 and 2010. As mentioned in the Gallup Poll quote, the limited data collected on the young adults in Generation Z shows their church activity is declining similarly to that of Millennials. Criticism of religion in general, a new skepticism towards establishments of any kind, and a desire to break conventions that have existed for millennia seem to be driving our two youngest generations away from church or any religious observance.[96]

With the older generations passing away and our younger generations not continuing in the faith, church attendance and activity are diminishing. Though disturbing, such news should not be surprising. Ours is The Church of Jesus Christ of *Latter-day* Saints. One can interpret the words "Latter-day" as distinguishing today's membership from that of the Church established by Jesus Christ two millennia ago. But most members understand that "Latter-day" communicates that we are in the latter days, or those just preceding the Second Coming. This situation was prophesized in the scriptures. In 1 Nephi chapter 14, Nephi recounts a vision he received regarding the last days. In 1 Nephi 14:12, Nephi sees the church of Jesus Christ and makes a single, disturbing comment about what he sees.

> And it came to pass that I beheld the church of the Lamb of God, and its numbers were few . . .

We are taught in the Church that the righteous will triumph in the end. For example, we sing the hymn "Hope of Israel," whose fourth verse reads,

> Soon the battle will be over;
> Ev'ry foe of truth be down.
> Onward, onward, youth of Zion;
> Thy reward the victor's crown.[97]

The hymn is accurate, in that the righteous will overcome in the end. However, the hymn does not mention the cost of that victory. There will be extensive collateral damage, which could include your friends and family who have left the Church. There is no evidence, scriptural or otherwise, of a revival of church activity and successful missionary work in the latter days. This is an unsettling conclusion. In talking with my son Trent about our diminishing church, he observed, "We are taught that the Church must be strong in the latter days. A stronger church may mean it will be a smaller church." His insight helped me to resolve some of my anxiety about that future.

What Will the Last Days Look Like?

4 Nephi

Generally, the Book of Revelation is the go-to scripture whenever one wants to discuss the days before the Second Coming. However, I am too literal of a person to enjoy reading Revelation. The books of 4 Nephi, Mormon, and Ether give more readable descriptions of what to expect in the last days. The paths of the rebellious Nephites and Jaredites were nearly identical and consisted of four steps. Turning to 4 Nephi, we read about the first step to destruction.

> . . . And the more wicked part of the people did wax strong, and became exceedingly more numerous than were the people of God. (4 Nephi 1:40)

Step 1—The number of people who deny God and refuse to follow His commandments becomes greater than faithful believers. There are a few ways to number these two groups. For example, through simple polls we know that many more people stay home from church on Sunday than attend worship services. We also find fewer people trying to live the law of chastity.

Continuing in 4 Nephi, we read about the second step.

> And it came to pass that the wicked part of the people began again to build up the secret oaths and combinations of Gadianton. (4 Nephi 1:42)

Step 2—Those people who deny God become even more wicked, turning to criminal acts to gain power and money. This increase is gradual of course. However, by comparing our present situation to a few decades ago, we can observe this decline too.

This increase in the more wicked part of the people has its effects on the rest of the population, as unrighteousness consumes nearly everyone. We continue to read,

> And also the people who were called the people of Nephi began to be proud in their hearts, because of their exceeding riches, and become vain like unto their brethren, the Lamanites.
>
> And from this time the disciples began to sorrow for the sins of the world. (4 Nephi 1:43–44)

Step 3—Until this step, the Nephites had not yet passed a point of no return. Earlier in their history, they had come back from the brink of such disasters. But not this time. Many of those who had followed Jesus Christ gradually turned away from Him. The pressures of their society were simply too much for them to endure. At this point, there are still pockets of true worshipers of the Savior, but they are becoming an ever-smaller minority. This is a significant turning point for the Nephites. The disciples recognized that fact and began to "sorrow for the sins of the world." Obviously, they had sorrowed for the sins of the world previously, but at this point it had become a deeper, more hopeless sorrow.

Just a couple of verses later, we read of the last step in the process.

> And it came to pass that when three hundred years had passed away, both the people of Nephi and the Lamanites had become exceedingly wicked one like unto another.
>
> And it came to pass that the robbers of Gadianton did spread over all the face of the land; and there were none that were righteous save it were the disciples of Jesus. (4 Nephi 1:45–46)

Step 4—Essentially everyone but a diminished number of disciples continue down the road of wickedness. It may be helpful at this point to note that the downfall of the Nephites began in about AD 200 (1 Nephi 1:24) and reached step 4 in AD 320 (1 Nephi 1:48). So, it took 120 years for this all to occur. As members of The Church of Jesus Christ of *Latter-day* Saints, we already knew that we are in a countdown mode for the Second Coming. We just don't know when the countdown officially started or when it will end.

The Book of Ether

The book of Ether is also a depressing read, as it is very similar to Mormon chapters 1–8. It too follows the same four steps to destruction followed by the Nephites. Step 3, the point of no return for the Jaredites, is given in Ether 11.

> And it came to pass that the people hardened their hearts, and would not hearken unto their words; and the prophets mourned and withdrew from among the people. (Ether 11:13)

It is a bad sign for a people when their prophets find it necessary to withdraw from among them. From this time until the final downfall of the Jaredites, we can count four generations—Ethem, Moron, Coriantor, and Ether. Approximating that each generation lasts 20–25 years, we are looking at 80–100 years from the time the people stopped listening to the prophets to the time of their destruction. Again, we know we are in a countdown; we just don't know where we are in it.

Ether was one of the prophets who came forth in what was apparently a last-ditch effort to reclaim the Jaredites. Ether's cries of repentance were never heeded by the people. As it turns out, his major role was to observe and document the destruction of the Jaredites, so that future peoples might take heed and not follow in their same path.

If you were to have seen the lands of the Nephites or the Jaredites after their wars, I expect the destructions described in the Book of Revelation would appear redundant. Death, destruction, fire, famine, and homelessness certainly followed the great wars of these two civilizations. The fulfillment of the Book of Revelation could hardly be much worse. What can we learn from the last days of these two peoples, recorded for us in the Book of Mormon?

The Spirit of the Lord Must Continue to Strive with Us

The point of this chapter rests on the fact that the last days will require applying the wisdom of the serpent while still pursuing the spiritual gifts of the dove. If our last days follow the same path as the Nephites and Jaredites, the blessings of the Spirit will be in short supply. Regarding the Nephites, we read in Mormon chapter 5,

> For behold, the Spirit of the Lord hath already ceased to strive with their fathers; and they are without Christ and God in the world; and they are driven about as chaff before the wind. (Mormon 5:16)

Something very similar occurred to the Jaredites, as we read in Ether,

> But behold, the Spirit of the Lord had ceased striving with them, and Satan had full power over the hearts of the people; for they were given up unto the hardness of their hearts . . . (Ether 15:19)

The people completely lost the dovelike side of their lives. They still had the serpentlike wile to survive in their difficulties, but their balance was completely gone. Such a loss is probably a gradual process, but one that we should be able to recognize in our day. The Spirit will stop striving to influence those people who continually ignore it, even if they include your family, neighbors, and dear friends. Without the Spirit, friends may turn away from principles they once held dear. They may try to distract you away from them too. We have learned enough about the Second Coming to know to expect this separation. It is occurring today. Our serpent side knows to expect that separation and brace ourselves to deal with it. Our dove side will provide us the love and forgiveness that will be required to maintain our relationships despite the challenges.

Sorting Out the Truth

We live in a disturbing time when falsehoods masquerade as truth. Within the realm of public debate, if you want to get people to believe a lie, you should include it in your argument with several truths. In his book *100 Signs of the Times*, David Ridges lists one hundred signs of the last days, many of which are in progress today. Some of these signs are how deceptions, which are obviously nonsense, will be accepted by many people as truth. Ridges's sign #65 states that "People will Refuse to Believe Obvious Truth and Will Adhere to Fables and Falsehoods."[98] Brother Ridges quotes from 2 Timothy chapter 4,

> For the time will come when they will not endure sound doctrine; but after their own lusts shall they heap to themselves teachers, having itching ears;
>
> And they shall turn away their ears from the truth, and shall be turned unto fables. (2 Timothy 4:3–4)

Many simple, basic truths, which have been accepted for decades, are under attack today. We are told that the traditional family unit is no longer the best organization within which to raise children. It is argued that there is no such thing as absolute truth. Others assure us that moral standards and values are outdated and have no place in today's world. Yet truth has not changed, despite the numbers of people arguing against it.

Most people dislike change and will deny the need for it as long as possible. We do not want to recognize that our old life is changing, because we enjoyed that life so very much. The Church of Jesus Christ of Latter-day Saints has made multiple changes, especially in the years since Russell M. Nelson became its president. Some of those changes were made in response to complaints by departing members. Others were made in response to COVID-19 and yet others to better recognize the roles of women. These changes have affected our Sunday meetings, our temple worship, missionary work, and almost every other aspect of our worship. The changes are a result of the Church trying to adapt with the times, maintain a good public image, and still maintain its principles and doctrine.

The Church will do all it can to be spiritually and financially prepared for the future. However, even such preparations will be criticized. For example, in late 2019, it was revealed that the Church had saved about $100 billion in its investments for future financial needs. The man who reported this news was called a whistleblower, and the article generated both criticism and suspicion.[99] Whether the article was accurate or not, shouldn't we be glad to hear that the Church is preparing for the worst of days? Yet critics imply that the Church is somehow doing something illegal in their investments. The problem with that criticism is that it has no place to go. Which Church authorities are living in sumptuous luxury? Which Church leaders have multimillion-dollar estates? The Church tries to manage its income wisely—and it is certainly not overpaying its leaders. Desperate days lie ahead, and those funds will be sorely needed.

This chapter was not meant to be a depressing reminder of the Second Coming. I think we have some time yet. However, the threats to righteous living by an increasingly secular world are great. We need our serpent side to calmly recognize, assess, and plan our response to those changes. We then need our dove side to seek the Spirit and increase our prayers both for ourselves and for those we love.

Chapter 24

If Any of You Lack Wisdom . . .

We have discussed how members of The Church of Jesus Christ of Latter-day Saints need to have the wisdom of the serpent. Part of that wisdom includes a very healthy dose of self-evaluation and humility. There are several verses about deceiving oneself, mostly written by the apostle Paul and found in the New Testament.

Before discussing these verses, we need to review a little history about Paul. Paul was, of course, converted to the gospel by a visit from the Savior as he traveled from Jerusalem to Damascus (Acts 9:1–4). Paul then becomes the most traveled missionary of the church.

Sometime during his travels, Paul found himself in Athens. Greece had been considered the center of learning for the civilized world for centuries. Aristotle, Plato, and Socrates all died between 400–300 BC, but their legacy lived on.

Yet Paul discovered Athens to be "wholly given to idolatry" (Acts 17:16). Still, several of the Greek philosophers and teachers were interested in hearing his message and booked him to speak on Mars Hill. Paul took the opportunity to chastise the gathered assembly about worshipping numerous gods. The Greeks had gone so far as to erect an altar to "the Unknown God," just in case they had missed one. Though a few people believed his words, Paul's talk was not well received. We read,

> And when they heard of the resurrection of the dead, some mocked: and others said, We will hear thee again of this matter.
>
> So Paul departed from among them. (Acts 17:32–33)

Paul never really liked Greek culture after that experience and criticized it in future letters. Granted, he found enough success in Greece to convert followers in Corinth, Thessaloniki, Ephesus, and Philippi. From his visits,

Paul recognized that there are two forms of wisdom. In fact, Paul's letters can be confusing, as you will find that he calls for wisdom in one verse and dismisses it as foolishness in another. He calls the wisdom of the Greeks the "wisdom of the world" or the "wisdom of the flesh."

> For it is written, I will destroy the wisdom of the wise, and will bring to nothing the understanding of the prudent. Where is the wise? where is the scribe? where is the disputer of this world? hath not God made foolish the wisdom of this world? For the Jews require a sign, and the Greeks seek after wisdom: But we preach Christ crucified, unto the Jews a stumblingblock, and *unto the Greeks foolishness.* (1 Corinthians 1:19–21, 22-23, italics added)

> For our rejoicing is this, the testimony of our conscience, that in simplicity and godly sincerity, not with *fleshly wisdom*, but by the grace of God . . . (2 Corinthians 1:12, italics added)

The greatest danger of seeking the wisdom of the serpent is finding the wisdom of the world instead. Self-deception is easy. We are taught to read scriptures, books on doctrine, Church history, and philosophical writings to increase our wisdom. Yet, there are thousands of different conclusions we can make from these studies. Then, being impressed with our own insights, we hold onto our beliefs tightly, refusing to consider that we might be in error. In my discussions with Church members over the years, I have heard interpretations of doctrine and Church history that contradict the most basic tenets of our religion. Fellow Church members have told me of their dreams which they were sure should be publicized to the entire Church.

Actually, this was the condition of the leaders of the Jewish religion that Jesus Christ found as He started His mission. The rabbis and chief priests of the Jewish religion were so impressed with their wisdom of the Mosaic Law, that they could not recognize the very Savior for whom they had waited for centuries. They were educated in the details of ritual sanitation and other minutia of their law, but had no understanding of the ways of their God. They simply couldn't see the bigger picture.

Do Not Fear to Seek Wisdom

However, we should never fear to seek more wisdom. For many years, some Latter-day Saints feared to attend scripture study groups outside of normal Church services. One member friend explained that, in such discussion groups, faithful Church members can end up "thinking their way right out of the Church." The implication was that, if you seek knowledge of Latter-day Saint doctrine or think about it too deeply, you will eventually end up leaving the religion. I have read too many scriptures and heard too many general conference talks that encourage me to seek wisdom to believe that.

The problem may be that we do not understand Paul's teachings of the differentiation of the wisdom of the world and the wisdom of God. For example, Paul teaches the Corinthians to *not* seek the pretentious wisdom of the Greeks, but that of God.

> Let no man deceive himself. If any man among you seemeth to be wise in this world, let him become a fool, that he may be wise. (1 Corinthians 3:18)

In other words, if you are wise with the wisdom of the world, start over and become a fool so you can then gain the wisdom of God. Now reading Paul's admonition to the Colossians,

> Beware lest any man spoil you through philosophy and vain deceit, after the tradition of men, after the rudiments of the world, and not after Christ. (Colossians 2:8)

The apostle James gave even more specific advice in his letter. First, James confirms the importance of wisdom by writing the verse that motivated Joseph Smith to go pray in the Sacred Grove.

> If any of you lack wisdom, let him ask of God, that giveth to all men liberally, and upbraideth not; and it shall be given him. (James 1:5)

Then James explains the difference between finding wisdom and deceiving yourself that you've found it. He states that if members hear the gospel but don't live it, they deceive themselves regarding their actual righteousness. We read,

> But be ye doers of the word, and not hearers only, deceiving your own selves. (James 1:22)

James then gave his readers a second way to recognize someone who is deceiving himself about his own heart or wisdom. If a Church member seems pious, but is unable to be careful in what he says, the man is deceiving himself that he is truly religious. Again we read from the first chapter of James,

> If any man among you seem to be religious, and bridleth not his tongue, but deceiveth his own heart, this man's religion is vain. (James 1:26)

So, for what wisdom should you seek? What is the end goal of lifelong study? I would suggest that wisdom includes:

1. Learning all we can about our physical and spiritual worlds and how they interact.
2. Learning all we can about other people.
3. Learning all we can about ourselves.

Learning about Our Physical and Spiritual Worlds

First, we should endeavor to learn all we can about our present reality, both the physical and the spiritual sides of it. We have two large groups of exceptionally smart people who study the universe and everything in it. One group is made up of astronomers, geologists, evolutionary biologists, and other scientists who seek to understand the physical laws and history of nature. These are fascinating fields, generating great discoveries of truths never before understood.

The second group of smart people is made up of theologists, clergy, and other students of religion. They study the spiritual side of our world. These two groups don't normally work well together. Neither group sees the value of the other's work, rather like the serpent and dove sides of our attitudes.

Yet, truth is truth—any precept or claim must ultimately make sense in our physical world and in the spiritual world. I am constantly amazed that some scientists and theologists believe in fortune-telling, astrology, ghosts, voodoo, and magic in general. Such things cannot be truth. Please note, there are numerous miracles in the scriptures, but they are not magic. Jesus's miracles all obeyed the laws of nature. However, as a god, Jesus knew much more than us about those laws of nature, so He knew how to circumvent them when the need arose.

Understanding how the physical world and the spiritual world interact strengthens one's testimony tremendously. My spiritual and my scientific understandings of the creation of the universe and God's role in it are both required to make sense of our existence. Losing my spiritual testimony means revising my whole understanding of the universe and how it came to be. It is too much work to rewrite everything I have learned about earth life since kindergarten. That fact will help keep my testimony in place for a long time.

Learning about Other People

About twelve years ago, the public became interested in learning to read other people's body language. Several books and a few television shows (e.g., *The Mentalist, Lie to Me*) resulted. I enjoyed watching those shows and even read a couple of the books about it. The ability to watch and listen to a person to determine their mood, mindset, and inner thoughts is fascinating.

Indeed, we need to develop wisdom in dealing with other people. Whether we are doing missionary work, counseling youth, or trying to keep peace in our family, we need to be able to read and empathize with people. We are given ward and stake callings to help us develop skills in leading, following, cooperating, and communicating.

To be a student of people, one must be willing to observe people. First, observe your own family. You should know them well, but quiet observation may help you judge how they are coping with life at the moment. You can then be more insightful as to what your loved one needs, be it an offer of help, some flowers, or a quart of their favorite ice cream. You can do the same thing with people at work or in your neighborhood. Observe. Conclude. Act. When you use your knowledge to help someone else, your understanding increases your wisdom.

At the same time, we must employ the wisdom of the serpent as we interact with our family and friends. I have seen many families in which one member is causing havoc and dysfunctionality within the rest of family. This realization is difficult, and the solution to the problem is challenging. It is difficult for families to admit that a close relative has gone off the rails and may need help. Our dove side wants to dwell on the good news of our relationships with family and friends. It is usually up to your serpent side to face the more disturbing facts of our relationships—and then devise a solution where possible. It is not an easy task; people are messy.

Learning about Your True Self

Once we have a beginning awareness of the universe, you must then seek to understand our place in it. Much of your "place in the world" is arranged by chance. For example, you were born into a particular family, and they had a significant effect on the person you are today. Some of your place in the world is set by your own decisions. You decide on your career, who you marry, and where you live. Some of your situation is set by a both chance and choice. You decided to have children, but you didn't get to choose them. Recognizing your place in the world and understanding who you are is a necessary step towards true wisdom.

This sounds easy enough. Yet, we live in a very confusing time when people are struggling to decide who they are. Today there are many people who are seeking to define their identity through their sexual preferences. This seems a strange development in our society. We are more familiar with people identifying themselves through their careers, marital and family status, hobbies, political affiliations, etc. To have so many people willing to publicize their sexual preferences as a part of their self-identification seems to be an indicator of a general confusion about understanding ourselves.

Many people talk about "finding their true selves" and "living their best lives." Such statements can lead to you making good decisions and getting your life in order. Or they might lead you to justify your choice of a new and enticing lifestyle that ruins your life and relationships with family. Here is where self-understanding is required. It is difficult to feel special or unique in a world of eight billion people, and many people ruin their lives in the effort. Please remember that your mind will rationalize its decisions and excuse itself from poor outcomes. If you want to find wisdom in understanding your place in the universe—as a spouse, parent, child, employee, church member, bicycling enthusiast, or whatever—be prepared to spend some time in honest self-evaluation.

This is not as easy as it may sound. I have had friends who advised me that they decided to simplify their lives by forgoing their activity in the Church. I have known men who decided to leave their wives and families. I have known young people who have decided to leave the stabilizing home of one parent to live with their other parent who consistently acts irresponsibly. The wisdom to understand your place in the universe sounds easy enough. Yet, it is not. Your self-image and self-esteem change every day. You must have the wisdom to act on the promptings that encourage you towards greatness—in your eyes, your family's eyes, and in God's eyes.

Chapter 25

Being Prepared for the End

My father passed away a few months ago. His passing was a blessing, as his physical and mental health had both seriously declined. He couldn't really communicate anymore. Yet in my last few days with him, for the first time ever, I saw a desperate terror in his eyes. My father was not a religious man and thought little about his death or the afterlife. In the end, he was urgently seeking reassurance that everything would be okay, because he had never prepared himself for this one inevitable moment. I vowed then to never be unprepared for my own death.

We need the wisdom of the serpent more in our elderly years than at any other time in our lives. Many elderly people refuse to recognize that their turn on Earth is almost over—yet they need to make plans for that eventuality. It is also very common for adult children to deny that their parents will be dying soon. When those parents are also in active denial, then preparations for the event never occur.

There are a couple of books, written by medical doctors, pleading with families to have discussions about living wills and death. I highly recommend both books. One is called *The Conversation* by Dr. Angelo E. Volandes.[100] The other is *Being Mortal* by Dr. Atul Gawande.[101] Both doctors were saddened by the number of elderly patients who were barely holding onto a bedridden, highly medicated, semiconscious existence, with no real chance of recovery. These patients had no living will or adult children who would agree to release them from this life. Their books are pleas to families to have the difficult conversations to prevent this sad semblance of life being afflicted on an elderly parent. The gentle, dove side of you may refuse to make such a difficult decision—but your serpent side should recognize the inevitable need and act upon it.

So, as you look at the years you have left on this world, what are your priorities? Your turn on Earth is almost over. What more do you need to do? How can the wisdom of the serpent be of use to you today?

Kung Fu

There was an old television series I watched in my youth. Aired from 1972–1975, the show was called *Kung Fu*.[102] It starred David Carradine as a Kwai Chang Caine, a Chinese Shaolin priest who travelled to the Wild West of America in the 1870s. Caine travelled about the country seeking to find his brother. Being a Shaolin priest of Buddhism, Caine practiced meditation and followed the dictates of his Far Eastern religion. Besides dealing with the racism of his time, Caine tried to help the poor and downtrodden, often having to physically defend them in the process. Fortunately, Caine was a master in the Chinese martial art called Kung Fu.

Despite his attempts to keep a low profile, in every episode Caine encountered a group of scoundrels who were persecuting innocent people. Every week, our hero had to kick and punch out those bad guys. Viewers watched the program for its action scenes of course. But the background message was interesting. Every week, this humble and quiet Chinese man, who was just trying to live a spiritual life, was dragged back into a world of violence where the strong oppress the weak. With a little reflection, such a life sets a pretty good example for what we should be seeking. On one hand, Caine was pursuing his spiritual goals of understanding the universe and the people around him. Yet he still helped those people who were in need of that help. Shouldn't that be the ultimate goal of anyone's life?

Being Prepared

We have already discussed the underlying reasons for religion. In the end, church worship is designed to make us better people. As an aside, there are few activities that try to accomplish such a task. Yet almost everyone wants your time and attention.

For example, social media wants as much time as you will give it. Every social media outlet wants you to visit their site and stay there for as long as possible. Social outlets continually suggest that you add more people to your "friends" list so that you can receive even more posts. This allows them to sell more marketing space to advertisers. With their posts, consumers can feel that that their voice is being heard. The videos you watch and the posts you read are all fed to you by a social media outlet that knows who you are and what you want to hear. Social media exists to take your time.

Politics will also take as much time as you are willing to give. In fact, today, you can have 24/7 news coverage. Political debates and commentary can occupy hours of your personal life if you let them. Whether you are Republican, Democrat, or Independent, your party wants your vote, your devotion to their platform, and your donations.

Your church and religion also want some of your time, encouraging you to attend Sunday services and carry out your callings. For religion, however, you are not simply a means to an end—you *are* the end goal. The goal is not to get you to vote a certain way, buy a certain product, or to hook you into a social media site and keep you there. The goal of Christian religion is to help you become a wiser and more capable person. Through my callings over the years, I have learned how to interact with toddlers, youth, adults, and the elderly. I feel I am prepared to interact with people of almost any age or background.

However, because it wants to help you to improve yourself, the Church can become very unpopular with many people. To get you to make improvements in your life, religions continually teach self-discipline and *change.* Yet . . . many people don't want to be told to change. They see the commandments as restrictive and the Church as being overbearing. Such people fight against the Church, not understanding that the changes sought are constructive.

There has been a backlash against churches and any kind of restrictions on behavior. Many people now believe they can manage their own spiritual development without the help of church or anyone else. To understand today's spiritual landscape, we need to know about this trend.

Spiritual, but Not Religious

Today we are told by our society that everyone is fine just the way they are. There should be no outside encouragement to become more understanding, socially mature, wiser, or more spiritual.

It is a popular belief that one's spirituality doesn't require any effort. Using polls, the Pew Foundation asks people about religion, including the question, "Do you consider yourself to be a spiritual person?" A favorite reply to this question has become "I am Spiritual but not Religious." In fact, over a quarter of US adults (27%) now say they think of themselves as "spiritual but not religious," up eight percentage points in five years. Not surprisingly, many in the "spiritual but not religious" category report low levels of religious observance, seldom or never attending religious services.[103]

The logic behind this belief is lacking. As Lillian Daniel, Pastor at 1st Congregational Church of Dubuque, Iowa expressed in her paper "Spiritual But Not Religious? Please Stop Boring Me,"

> On airplanes, I dread the conversation with the person who finds out I am a minister and wants to use the flight time to explain to me that he is "spiritual but not religious." Such a person will always share this as if it is some kind of daring insight, unique to him, bold in its rebellion against the religious status quo.
>
> Next thing you know, he's telling me that he finds God in the sunsets. These people always find God in the sunsets. And in walks on the beach.[104]

In the face of such self-delusion, Pastor Daniel's sarcasm is understandable, and I agree with her observation. How can you become more spiritual without following God's commands to keep the Sabbath day holy and observe religious precepts? One doesn't gain spirituality or other noble characteristics by simply thinking about them. They take work, effort, and help from others in your faith. A lifetime is barely enough time to accomplish such a task.

THE AFTERLIFE

Strangely enough, many people who ignore their spiritual development still believe in some form of an afterlife. They realize they can't take their big houses, boats, or money with them when they die. Often, they comprehend that there will be some form of judgment. Yet these understandings do not help them find motivation to become more spiritual.

In the Final Judgment, you probably won't be judged for every good deed, bad move, or act of repentance accomplished over the decades of your life. Those actions will be collectively imprinted upon your spirit. Your kindness, charity, spirituality, and wisdom will finally be visible. In fact, your Heavenly Father should be able to judge you with His very first glance. He will be able to see the effects of your family circumstances, gifts, opportunities, and challenges.

One can compare a premortal spirit with a new journal with only a few written pages at the very beginning. That spirit doesn't exist anymore. It has been added to and, very probably, overwritten in parts. Yet, until you pass away, the journal is not complete. It takes the brutal honesty of the serpent to conduct the self-assessments required to recognize what more you can be doing to improve. As we enter our elderly years and approach our own deaths, we must know that we can enhance the endings of our stories. We must continually assess what is left for us to accomplish.

To conclude this chapter encouraging us to be wise as serpents and spiritual as doves, I would like to offer up the following quotes.

> Exercise caution in your business affairs; for the *world is full of trickery*. But let this not blind you to what *virtue there is*; many persons strive for high ideals; and everywhere life is full of heroism. (Desiderata, italics added)[105]

> For they that *are wise* and have received the truth, and have for their guide, and *have not been deceived*—verily I say unto you, they shall not be hewn down and cast into the fire, but shall *abide the day*. (D&C 45:57, italics added)

> Therefore, be ye *wise as serpents* and *yet without sin*, and I will order all things for your good, as fast as ye are able to receive them. Amen. (D&C 111:11, italics added)

Chapter 26

Peter's Journey

In the early part of the Savior's ministry, the apostle Peter didn't really stand out as a potential leader within the quorum. He was allowed to go up the Mount of Transfiguration to see Moses and Elias, but otherwise he didn't set himself apart as an example of competence and good judgment. In fact, at the end of Christ's ministry, Peter hit a particularly rough stretch and seemed unable to get anything right.

First, Peter tried to dissuade Jesus from going to Jerusalem at all, knowing enough to be certain that danger awaited them there. In Matthew 16, Jesus responded to Peter,

> Get thee behind me, Satan: thou art an offence unto me: for thou savourest not the things that be of God, but those that be of men. (Matthew 16:23)

Ouch. This was the kind of rebuke Jesus Christ usually saved for the scribes and Pharisees. He had used the same exact wording to chastise Satan when the devil was trying to tempt the Savior with power to abandon his earthly purpose (Luke 4:8).

When Jesus and His apostles arrive in Jerusalem, they found and entered the room they had reserved for the Last Supper. Jesus started washing His apostles' feet, which confused Peter. We read,

> Peter saith unto him, Thou shalt never wash my feet. Jesus answered him, If I wash thee not, thou hast no part with me. (John 13:8)

Peter immediately told the Savior He could wash his feet, hands, and head if He wanted. Peter didn't understand that Jesus's washing of the feet was a symbol to demonstrate that all should be servants to each other. This was more than just a foot bath. Peter had not looked beyond the simple act of service by the Savior to understand the message behind it.

Later that evening, when the Romans and Jewish leaders appeared to arrest Jesus in the Garden of Gethsemane, Peter drew out a sword and cut off a servant's ear. According to John 18, as He healed the man's ear, Jesus harshly rebuked Peter yet again,

> Then said Jesus unto Peter, Put up thy sword into the sheath: the cup which my Father hath given me, shall I not drink it? (John 18:11)

In recounting this same event, Matthew recorded more of what Jesus said to Peter to get him to understand what was happening. We read,

> Thinkest thou that I cannot now pray to my Father, and he shall presently give me more than twelve legions of angels?
>
> But how then shall the scriptures be fulfilled, that thus it must be? (Matthew 26:53–54)

Peter was just not getting it. Because of his misunderstandings and protective love for the Savior, Peter was working at cross purposes to the Savior's plan. He didn't comprehend the sacrifice that the new gospel law required of the Savior. Yet, after all of this, the worst night of Peter's life was not over. While eating their Passover dinner, Jesus had told Peter that he would deny him three times before the night's end. Peter vehemently denied the charge, stating he would die first. Yet, sure enough, after Jesus's arrest, Peter denied knowing the Savior three times in a row. From the accusations that Peter was a follower of Jesus, Peter probably feared for his own life. He didn't seem to realize he was fulfilling prophecy until right after his third denial.

> And Peter remembered the word of Jesus, which said unto him, Before the cock crow, thou shalt deny me thrice. And he went out, and wept bitterly. (Matthew 26:75)

Jesus Christ had made enough references to His resurrection that the apostles should have probably been expecting it. Even the Jewish leaders knew about the claim. The chief priests and Pharisees met with Pilate to remind him that Jesus had said that He would arise after three days. They wanted Pilate to post a watch to prevent someone from stealing the body and claiming there had been a resurrection. Despite the teachings that the Savior had given His apostles, they were still rather obviously unprepared for the Resurrection. After Mary Magdalene and her friends first announced

Jesus's absence from the tomb, they didn't believe her. Finally, they ran to the tomb to see for themselves. We read about Peter's reaction in Luke 24.

> Then arose Peter, and ran unto the sepulchre; and stooping down, he beheld the linen clothes laid by themselves, and departed, wondering in himself at that which was come to pass. (Luke 24:12)

After the arrest, crucifixion, and resurrection, Peter continued to be unaware of his responsibilities. With Jesus gone, Peter decided to return to his previous occupation, as we read in John 21.

> Simon Peter saith unto them, I go a fishing. They say unto him, We also go with thee. They went forth, and entered into a ship immediately; and that night they caught nothing.
>
> But when the morning was now come, Jesus stood on the shore: but the disciples knew not that it was Jesus. (John 21:3–4)

This was the third time the apostles were visited by the resurrected Savior. Nonetheless, Peter jumped into the water to wade to shore and greet his Master. The group settled down for a dinner of fish and bread. Afterwards, Jesus asked Peter if he loved Him. At Peter's affirmative response, Jesus told him, "Feed my sheep." Jesus repeated this question and directive two more times to make sure Peter understood that He wanted Peter to lead His church.

Peter's Learnings

If you have ever had a really hard time in your life, where you just keep making one mistake after another, please know that the great man who succeeded the Savior as leader of His church had it worse. Peter went through a period of intense learning, mostly requiring him to gain the wisdom of the serpent and be ready to lead the fledgling church of Jesus Christ. We can see what Peter learned from each of his goofs.

Peter tried to dissuade Jesus from going to Jerusalem. In the Savior's stinging chastisement, Peter was taught that doing the things of God can be difficult, but they must be faced and endured. Often, it takes courage to follow God. Then Peter didn't want the Savior to wash his feet. In His response, Jesus taught him that everyone, including leadership, was to serve everyone else. The next President of the Church, especially needed to understand that.

After the arrest, Peter denied knowing the Savior three times over the course of a few hours. When he realized what he had done, Peter wept bitterly.

He would never forget this experience, never forget how his fear had overcome his loyalty and dedication to the Savior. Peter needed to look his fear in the face and understand what it had caused him to do. Through the rest of the New Testament, Peter never allowed personal fear to affect his decisions.

Peter cut off a servant's ear when the Romans and Jewish leaders came to arrest Jesus. Once again, the Savior had to rebuke Peter for trying to stop His arrest and crucifixion. The Savior could have stopped it, but He wouldn't. In the Church of Jesus Christ, we may be asked to accomplish difficult things. We must face and meet the expectations of God. Peter needed to face reality and stop delaying what needed to be done.

Next, Peter found the empty tomb and realized that the Savior had been resurrected, just as He had indicated He would be. Peter needed a lesson in believing prophecy and appreciating the power of God over death. Until he saw the empty tomb, it does not appear that Peter understood the significance of the Savior's life or His death.

Finally, Peter and his friends decided to . . . . go back to fishing. It appears that Peter was returning to his old profession because he didn't know what else to do. Yet, again, it was the wrong decision. Jesus visited His apostles to make it clear to Peter that he was supposed to lead the Church. This was probably a rather overwhelming reality check for Peter. He was called to take over the leadership role of the Savior's church. Once he finally understood the need, Peter accepted the calling, as we knew he would.

Yet the Savior had one more harsh reality check for His apostle. Apparently, He wanted Peter to know everything that was in store for him. Peter was to become the prophet and leader of the fledgling Church of Jesus Christ—and then he would "stretch forth his hands" and be crucified as was Jesus.[106] We read the Savior's words to Peter in John 21.

> Verily, verily, I say unto thee, When thou wast young, thou girdedst thyself, and walkedst whither thou wouldest: but when thou shalt be old, thou shalt stretch forth thy hands, and another shall gird thee, and carry thee whither thou wouldest not.
>
> This spake he, signifying by what death he should glorify God. And when he had spoken this, he saith unto him, Follow me. (John 21:18–19)

Peter needed this time of brutal instruction to become the leader of the Church. Peter desperately needed the practical wisdom of the serpent to do this. He needed to learn to not be naïve nor impulsive, but to be the new leader and teacher of the Church of Jesus Christ. Peter knew how his life would end, a foreknowledge he later revealed in one of his letters (2 Peter 1:14). After Peter had learned so much over these last days of the Savior's ministry, Jesus concluded His final admonition to Peter with the two words, "Follow me."

Our Own Journeys

Like Peter, The Church of Jesus Christ of Latter-day Saints will be facing its own difficult realities in the coming years. We can't be naïve about the challenges we face as its membership. We must continue to be like the dove—gentle, caring, and meek. In fact, this should be our go-to attitude in our dealings with other people. However, in our efforts to be accommodating and polite to others, we should not allow them to bump us off our own path of righteousness and church attendance. We need to actively preserve our testimonies. We should be aware of the fatal flaws behind criticisms and attacks of the Church. As parents, we must candidly discuss with our children the challenges they are facing. As youth in the Church, staying worthy, fulfilling a mission, or making temple covenants is not a simple rite of passage any longer. These accomplishments require resolve, courage, and a dedication to being righteous sons and daughters of God.

It should not come as a surprise that we aren't living in the "good old days" anymore. Much civility and many courtesies of that past have been lost. However, we are not yet living in the very last days filled with earthquakes, tempests, a blood-red moon, or a darkened sun. We are living in the days of active criticism of the Church and an exodus of our younger generations. Amidst the realities of present-day life, we can be reassured that Church doctrine is still based on the scriptures and revelation. Through it all, we need to maintain a dovelike love for our fellowman and a serpentlike awareness of the challenges and criticisms of our faith. The Church must survive to prepare the world for the Second Coming.

In conclusion, we live in a day when we must be aware of the Savior's warning, "Behold, I send you forth as sheep in the midst of wolves: be ye therefore wise as serpents, and harmless as doves" (Matthew 10:16). This instruction is more relevant to us today than it has ever been. We need to recognize and hone both those skills to face this new and changing world. May God bless you in your efforts to protect yourself, your family, and your eternities.

Endnotes

Introduction

1 Martin Luther King, Jr., *The Strength to Love* (Minneapolis: Fortress Press, 2010), 1–9.

2 David A. Bednar, "Prepared to Obtain Every Needful Thing," April 2019 General Conference, churchofjesuschrist.org.

PART 1

Chapter 1

3 Dennis Romboy, "Does Utah deserve the title 'fraud capital of the United States'?" Deseret News, 29 Apr. 2019, https://www.deseret.com/2019/4/29/20671965/does-utah-deserve-the-title-fraud-capital-of-the-united-states.

4 "Where Justice, Love, and Mercy Meet," *Media Library: Inspirational Messages—Missionary Teaching*, https://www.churchofjesuschrist.org/media/video/2017-01-001-where-justice-love-and-mercy-meet?lang=eng.

5 Jeffrey R. Holland, "Where Justice, Love, and Mercy Meet," April 2015 General Conference, churchofjesuschrist.org.

Chapter 2

6 "Religious Landscape Study: Generational Cohort," *Pew Research Center* (2014), accessed Feb. 2023, https://www.pewresearch.org/religion/religious-landscape-study/generational-cohort/.

Chapter 3

7 Richard Lyman Bushman, *Joseph Smith—Rough Stone Rolling* (New York: Vintage Books, 2005), 169.

8 Anthony Weston, *A Rulebook for Arguments* (Indianapolis, IN: Hackett Publishing Company, 2017), xiii.

9 "Under the Banner of Heaven: User Reviews," *IMDb*, https://www.imdb.com/title/tt1998372/reviews?ref_=tt_ov_rt

Chapter 4

10 Keith A. Erekson, *Real vs. Rumor, How to Dispel Latter-day Myths* (Salt Lake City, UT: Deseret Book Company, 2021), 51.

11 Michael R. Ash, *Bamboozled by the "CES Letter"* (CreateSpace Independent Publishing Platform, 2016).

12 Ross Winn, "2021 Podcast Stats & Facts (New research From Apr 2021)," *Podcast Insights,* 28 Dec. 2021, https://www.podcastinsights.com/podcast-statistics.

13 Coral Ouellette, "Ultimate List of Blogging Statistics and Facts (Updated for 2023), *optinmonster,* 22 Apr. 2022, https://optinmonster.com/blogging-statistics.

14 Neal A. Maxwell, "'Becometh As a Child,'" April 1996 General Conference, churchofjesuschrist.org.

Chapter 5

15 Cecelia Smith-Schoenwalder, "CDC: U.S. Coronavirus Death Toll to Top 200,000 by Sept. 26," *U.S. News,* 3 Sept. 2020, https://www.usnews.com/news/national-news/articles/2020-09-03/cdc-us-coronavirus-death-toll-to-top-200-000-by-sept-26.

16 "US Coronavirus vaccine tracker," *USA Facts,* updated 31 Aug. 2022, https://usafacts.org/visualizations/covid-vaccine-tracker-states/.

17 Belinda Luscombe, "Why Everyone Is So Rude Right Now," *Time,* 15 Oct. 2021, https://time.com/6099906/rude-customers-pandemic/.

18 Ibid.

19 Winston Churchill, speech to the House of Commons, 1948, retrieved from Quote.org, July 2023, https://quote.org/quote/those-who-fail-to-learn-from-history-645821.

20 Jonathan Haidt, *The Happiness Hypothesis: Finding Modern Truth in Ancient Wisdom* (New York: Basic Books, 2006), 17.

21 *Network,* directed by Sidney Lumet (United Artists, 1976).

Chapter 6

22 Paul Elsher, "Anecdotal Fallacy: Why Is The Use of Anecdotal Evidence Fallacious?", *Fallacy in Logic,* accessed Feb. 2023, https://fallacyinlogic.com/anecdotal-fallacy-definition-and-examples/.

23 Paul Elsher, "Hasty Generalization Fallacy: Definition And Examples," *Fallacy in Logic,* accessed Feb. 2023, https://fallacyinlogic.com/hasty-generalization-fallacy-definition-and-examples/.

24 "2021 Statistical Report for the April 2022 Conference," 2 Apr. 2022, *The Church of Jesus Christ of Latter-day Saints—Newsroom,* https://newsroom.churchofjesuschrist.org/article/2021-statistical-report-april-2022-conference.

Chapter 7

25 "The 2020 Census of American Religion," *PRRI,* 8 Jul. 2021, https://www.prri.org/research/2020-census-of-american-religion/.

26 Patrick Q. Mason, *Planted: Belief and Belonging in an Age of Doubt* (Salt Lake City, UT: Deseret Book, 2015), 12–15.

27 B.H. Roberts, *A Comprehensive History of the Church of Jesus Christ of Latter-day Saints,* Vol. 1, (Provo, UT: Brigham Young University Press, 1965), 128–130.

28 "Whitewash," *Merriam-Webster.com Dictionary,* accessed Feb. 2023, https://www.merriam-webster.com/dictionary/whitewash.

PART 2

Chapter 8

29 "Chapter 2: Of God, and of the Holy Trinity," *The Westminster Confession of Faith,* 2:1, 12 May 2021, https://www.ligonier.org/learn/articles/westminster-confession-faith.

30 "What the Early Church Believed: God Has No Body," *Catholic Answers,* accessed Feb. 2023, https://www.catholic.com/tract/god-has-no-body.

31 Joseph Smith History 1:18–19

Chapter 9

32 "America's Changing Religious Landscape," *Pew Research Center,* 12 May 2015,

https://www.pewresearch.org/religion/2015/05/12/americas-changing-religious-landscape/. See also, "In U.S., Decline of Christianity Continues at Rapid Pace," *Pew Research Center*, 17 Oct. 2019, https://www.pewresearch.org/religion/2019/10/17/in-u-s-decline-of-christianity-continues-at-rapid-pace/.

33 Jana Riess, *The Next Mormons* (New York: Oxford University Press, 2019), 17–19.

34 Quentin L. Cook, "Can Ye Feel So Now?" Oct. 2012 General Conference, churchofjesuschrist.org.

35 Dieter F. Uchtdorf, "Come, Join with Us," Oct. 2013 General Conference, churchofjesuschrist.org.

36 "Gospel Topics Essays," accessed Feb. 2023, https://www.churchofjesuschrist.org/study/manual/gospel-topics-essays/essays?lang=eng.

37 "Gospel Topics Essays: Contents," accessed Feb. 2023, https://www.churchofjesuschrist.org/study/manual/gospel-topics-essays?lang=eng.

Chapter 10

38 "Christian," *Dictionary.com*, accessed Feb. 2023, https://www.dictionary.com/browse/christian.

39 "Christian Definition," *YourDictionary*, accessed Feb. 2023, https://www.yourdictionary.com/christian.

Chapter 11

40 Joseph Smith—History 1:62–65

41 Richard E. Turley Jr., *Victims—The LDS Church and the Mark Hofmann Case* (University of Illinois Press, 1992), 296–297, 348.

42 Doctrine and Covenants, sections 66 & 68

43 Richard E. Turley, Jr., *Victims—The LDS Church and the Mark Hofmann Case* (University of Illinois Press, 1992), 185.

44 Dallin H. Oaks, "Recent Events Involving Church History and Forged Documents", *Ensign*, Oct. 1987, 63, churchofjesuschrist.org.

45 Richard E. Turley Jr., *Victims—The LDS Church and the Mark Hofmann Case* (University of Illinois Press, 1992), 343.

Chapter 12

46 Lorenzo Snow, "Chapter 5: The Grand Destiny of the Faithful," *Teachings of Presidents of the Church: Lorenzo Snow* (The Church of Jesus Christ of Latter-day Saints, 2012), 84.

47 "Mother in Heaven," *Gospel Topics Essays*, https://www.churchofjesuschrist.org/study/manual/gospel-topics-essays/mother-in-heaven?lang=eng.

Chapter 13

48 *Inherit the Wind*, produced by Stanley Kramer (United Artists, 1960).

49 "Book of Mormon and DNA Studies," *Gospel Topics Essays*, https://www.churchofjesuschrist.org/study/manual/gospel-topics-essays/book-of-mormon-and-dna-studies?lang=eng.

50 Elizabeth Baquedano, *Aztec, Inca, and Maya* (New York: DK Publishing, 2011), 9.

51 Ibid, 6.

52 Colin McEvedy & Richard Jones, *Atlas of World Population History* (Penguin Books, 1978), 294.

53 Eric A. Powell, "Oldest Maya Temple", *Archeology Magazine*, Jan./Feb. 2021, 34, https://www.archaeology.org/issues/407-2101/features/top10?start=5.

54 "Book of Mormon and DNA Studies," *Gospel Topics Essays,* https://www.churchofjesuschrist.org/study/manual/gospel-topics-essays/book-of-mormon-and-dna-studies?lang=eng.

55 D. Jeffrey Meldrum & Trent D. Stephens, *Who Are the Children of Lehi?* (Salt Lake City, UT: Greg Kofford Books, 2007), 46.

Chapter 14

56 "Presentism Definition," *YourDictionary,* accessed Feb. 2023, https://www.yourdictionary.com/presentism.

57 Richard Lyman Bushman, *Joseph Smith: Rough Stone Rolling* (New York: Vintage Books; Random House, 2005) 48–52.

58 Michael Hubbard Mackay & Nicholas J. Frederick, *Joseph Smith's Seer Stones* (Provo, UT: Brigham Young University, 2016), xii.

59 Ibid, 2.

60 Richard Lyman Bushman, *Joseph Smith Rough Stone Rolling* (New York: Alfred A. Knopf, 2005), 76–77.

Chapter 15

61 "translate," *Vocabulary.com*, accessed Feb. 2023, https://www.vocabulary.com/dictionary/translate.

62 Ibid.

63 Hugh Nibley, *Abraham in Egypt* (Salt Lake City, UT: Deseret Book, 1981), 3.

64 "Translation and Historicity of the Book of Abraham," *Gospel Topics Essays,* https://www.churchofjesuschrist.org/study/manual/gospel-topics-essays/translation-and-historicity-of-the-book-of-abraham?lang=eng.

65 Introduction to The Book of Abraham, Pearl of Great Price, https://www.churchofjesuschrist.org.

66 Nibley, *Abraham in Egypt*, 5–9.

67 Kerry Muhlestein, "The Explanation-Defying Book of Abraham" in *A Reason for Faith—Navigating LDS Doctrine and Church History*, ed. Laura Harris Hales, (Provo, UT: Religious Studies Center, BYU, 2016), 81.

68 Ibid, 81.

69 Nibley, *Abraham in Egypt*, 86.

70 Nibley, *Abraham in Egypt*, 111.

71 Don Bradley and Mark Ashurst-McGee, "Joseph Smith and the Kinderhook Plates," in Laura Harris Hales, ed., *A Reason for Faith: Navigating LDS Doctrine and Church History* (Provo, Utah: Religious Studies Center, Brigham Young University, 2016), 93–97.

72 Nibley, *Abraham in Egypt*, 10.

73 Nibley, Abraham in Egypt, 83.

74 Nibley, *Abraham in Egypt*, 13.

Chapter 16

75 Robert L. Millet, "What is Our Doctrine?" *Religious Educator* 4, #3 (2003), 15–33.

76 J. Reuben Clark, as quoted by Dennis B. Horne, *Determining Doctrine* (Roy, UT: Eborn Books, 2005), 158.

77 Bruce R. McConkie, as quoted in *Determining Doctrine* (Roy, UT: Eborn Books, 2005), 147.

Chapter 17

78 *Aladdin*, directed by John Musker and Ron Clements, (Walt Disney Studios, 1992).

79 Parley P. Pratt, Jr., *Autobiography of Parley P. Pratt* (Chicago: Law, King & Law, 1888), 329–330.

Chapter 18

80 Carol Lynn Pearson, *The Ghost of Eternal Polygamy* (Pivot Point Books, 2016); Ann Eliza Young, *Wife No. 19* (Illumination Publishing, 2016).

81 Solomon Schechter and Julius H. Greenstone, "Marriage Laws," *Jewish Encyclopedia.com*, accessed Feb. 2023, https://www.jewishencyclopedia.com/articles/10435-marriage-laws.

82 "Why Did Muhammad Have So Many Wives?" *Islam Online,* accessed Feb. 2023, https://islamonline.net/en/why-did-muhammad-have-so-many-wives/; Parvez Ahmed, "Muhammad's Wives: Background You Need to Know," *Orlando Sentinel,* 3 Dec. 2002, https://www.orlandosentinel.com/news/os-xpm-2002-12-04-0212040054-story.html.

83 Harry L. Munsinger, *The History of Marriage and Divorce* (Bloomington, IN: Archway Publishing, 2019) 17–22.

84 "Plural Marriage in Kirtland and Nauvoo," *Gospel Topics Essays,* https://www.churchofjesuschrist.org/study/manual/gospel-topics-essays/plural-marriage-in-kirtland-and-nauvoo?lang=eng.

Chapter 19

85 Aaron L. West, "Questions and Answers about the Temple Lot in Independence, Missouri," *The Church of Jesus Christ of Latter-day Saints*: Church History, 14 Mar. 2019, https://history.churchofjesuschrist.org/content/historic-sites/missouri/questions-and-answers-about-the-temple-lot-in-independence-missouri.

86 *Saints: The Story of the Church of Jesus Christ in the Latter Days, Volume 1, The Standard of Truth* (The Church of Jesus Christ of Latter-day Saints, 2018), 298–299.

87 Ibid, 571.

88 Ibid, 583.

89 James Talmage, *Jesus the Christ* (Salt Lake City, UT: Deseret Book Company, 1974), 528.

90 Richard Lyman Bushman, *Joseph Smith: Rough Stone Rolling* (New York: Vintage Books, Random House, 2005), 448.

91 Steven C. Harper, "Freemasonry and the Latter-day Saint Temple Endowment Ceremony" in *A Reason for Faith—Navigating LDS Doctrine and Church History,* ed. Laura Harris Hales, (Provo, UT: Religious Studies Center, BYU, 2016), 149–153; Matthew B. Brown, *Exploring the Connection between Mormons and Masons* (American Fork, UT: Covenant Communications, Inc., 2009), 114.

Chapter 20

92 Ty Mansfield, "Homosexuality and the Gospel" in *A Reason for Faith* (Provo, UT: Brigham Young University, 2016), 209.

PART 3

Chapter 22

93 The Church of Jesus Christ of Latter-day Saints, Bible Photographs, no. 3, "Judean wilderness."

Chapter 23

94 Jeffrey M. Jones, "U.S. Church Membership Falls Below Majority for First Time," *Gallup,* 29 Mar. 2021 https://news.gallup.com/poll/341963/church-membership-falls-below-majority-first-time.aspx

95 Jana Riess, *The Next Mormons* (New York: Oxford University Press, 2019), 17–19.

96 "Religious Landscape Study: Attendance at religious services," *Pew Research Center,* 2014, https://www.pewresearch.org/religion/religious-landscape-study/attendance-at-religious-services/.

97 "Hope of Israel," *Hymns,* no. 259, The Church of Jesus Christ of Latter-day Saints.

98 David Ridges, *100 Signs of the Times* (Springville, UT: Cedar Fort Inc., 2019), 209.

99 Peggy Fletcher Stack, "LDS Church kept the lid on its $100B fund for fear tithing receipts would fall, account boss tells Wall Street Journal," *The Salt Lake Tribune,* 8 Feb. 2020, https://www.sltrib.com/news/2020/02/08/lds-church-kept-lid-its-b/; Tad Walch, "Church responds to allegations made by former employee in IRS complaint," *Deseret News,* 17 Dec. 2019, https://www.deseret.com/utah/2019/12/17/21026182/mormon-lds-church-washington-post-whistleblower-irs-complaint-taxes-ensign-peak.

Chapter 25

100 Angelo E. Volandes, *The Conversation* (New York: Bloomsbury, 2015).

101 Atul Gawande, *Being Mortal* (New York: Picador, 2014).

102 *Kung Fu,* created by Ed Spielman, Jerry Thorpe, and Herman Miller (Warner Bros., 1972–1975), television series.

103 Michael Lipka and Claire Gegewicz, "More Americans now say they're spiritual and not religious," *Pew Research Center,* 6 Sept. 2017, https://www.pewresearch.org/fact-tank/2017/09/06/more-americans-now-say-theyre-spiritual-but-not-religious/.

104 Lillian Daniel, "Spiritual But Not Religious? Please Stop Boring Me.", *HuffPost,* 13 Nov. 2011, https://www.huffpost.com/entry/spiritual-but-not-religio_b_959216.

105 Max Ehrmann, "Desiderata," *The Poems of Max Ehrmann* (B. Humphries Publishing, 1948)

Chapter 26

106 James E. Talmage, *Jesus the Christ* (Salt Lake City, UT: Deseret Book, 1974), 693.

About the Author

Scott R. Frazer joined The Church of Jesus Christ of Latter-day Saints when he was nineteen years old and left on a mission to Mexico City a year later. Upon his return to Colorado, Scott married his wife Cheri and then earned his doctorate in Analytical Chemistry. His work history includes research and product development roles in a variety of fields.

Scott has published three other books, which apply the understandings of science to help us better comprehend the gospel and earth life. He produces a podcast called *Science and Scriptures* and maintains a website at scottrfrazer.com.

Scott and Cheri live in Saratoga Springs, Utah. They have four adult children and ten grandchildren.

Scan the QR code to
visit scottrfrazer.com